T0221715

ISRAELISM

Arab Scholarship
on Israel, a
Critical Assessment

ISRAELISM

Arab Scholarship on Israel, a Critical Assessment

Hassan A. Barari

ISRAELISM
Arab Scholarship on Israel, a Critical Assessment

Published by
Ithaca Press
8 Southern Court
South Street
Reading
RG1 4QS
UK

www.ithacapress.co.uk
www.twitter.com/Garnetpub
www.facebook.com/Garnetpub
thelevant.wordpress.com

Ithaca Press is an imprint of Garnet Publishing Limited.

First Paperback Edition

ISBN: 978-0-86372-416-9

British Library Cataloguing-in-Publication Data
A catalogue record for this book is available from the British Library

Typeset by Samantha Barden
Jacket design by Garnet Publishing

Printed and bound in Lebanon by International Press:
interpress@int-press.com

To my late parents

Contents

Acknowledgements

—-—

There are a number of individuals and institutions to whom I owe a debt of gratitude and without whose support this book would never have seen the light. First of all, I would like to extend my appreciation to the United States Institute of Peace (USIP) for granting me a senior fellowship for the year 2006–07 to write this book. I would like also to thank my colleagues at the Jennings Randolph Program for International Peace for their constant support, especially John Crist, Lynn Tesser, Judy Barsalou, Virginia Bourvier, Shira Lowinger, Erin Barrar, Scott Lasensky and Steven Heydemann.

My two research assistants, Christopher Neu and Dina Khanat (both are graduate students of Georgetown University), deserve special thanks for their continuous support, enthusiasm and constructive feedback. I am also grateful to my good friend from Egypt, Said Okasheh, for his help in sending me some material and for his passionate support of me during the period of writing this book.

All along my academic journey, my family in Jordan has been of great help. Undoubtedly, my family's love, support and trust in me is unparalleled and words cannot describe how much appreciation I have towards them. I am really fortunate to have them in my life. Karol Streit and Ivan Streit were also of great help during my stay in America and they deserve special thanks.

Last but not least, I owe a debt of gratitude to Lindsey Barari, for her genuine love, unfettered encouragement, generosity and passionate dedication that has made my otherwise difficult transition in the United States a pleasant adventure. She has lent a sense of purpose and deep understanding to the unpredictable demands of academia.

Introduction

— —

Israel has posed the greatest challenge to the Arab state system in the post-colonial Middle East. Hence, Israel occupies a central space in the daily debate that is taking place around the Arab world, which has clearly grappled, over the decades, with how it should respond to this challenge. The accompanying dispossession of hundreds of thousands of Palestinians who became refugees after the creation of Israel, and the persistence of violent Arab–Israeli interaction, has shaped the way Arab writers have previously dealt and continue to deal with Israel. These events have left a deep-seated mark on the collective Arab mindset. Against this backdrop, writing on Israel has not been objective and has been linked to the conflict prism, which has defined much of the epistemology and ontology of Israeli studies in the Arab world thus limiting the understanding of Israel as a topic for study.

I am, by training, a political scientist. I have studied wider Middle Eastern politics, but have focused much of my intellectual energy on the Arab–Israeli conflict and the peace process. Almost all of my scholarly writing has dealt, directly or indirectly, with Israel. In order to make sense of Israel's society and politics, and also positively contribute to the scholarship on Israel, I found it necessary to learn Hebrew. I have since read a good deal of Hebrew literature and consider myself a big fan of the Israeli novelist Amos Oz. I believe that my command of Arabic, English and Hebrew places me in an ideal situation to examine the conflict and the wider dynamic of the Middle East from an even-handed and unprejudiced perspective. I was determined right from the start to go beyond the intellectual confines of pan-Arabism and attempt to see things as they truly are.

Of equal importance, is the fact that I am an Arab who is very proud of his culture and historical legacy, yet I am open to other people, cultures and perspectives. I have read a great deal on our glorious past, particularly with regard to when the Arabs were the masters of world politics. The world has undergone a fundamental transformation at all levels over the last millennium. Throughout this time, the Arabs have been subject to varying forms of external pressures and colonization which have contributed to where we are today. Undoubtedly, the Arabs are lagging behind the Western world at all levels pertaining to human development. The majority in the Arab world attributes their decline, and what seems to be an age-old chronic stagnation, to external factors. However, while I acknowledge the destructive impact of external factors, I subscribe to the school of thought that contends that the reason for our contemporary underdevelopment is, by and large, internal. Sadly, many Arabs are in self-denial.

Before I embarked on what many would dub as a 'controversial' intellectual inquiry, I took a step back, thought thoroughly and asked myself what was it that I wanted to achieve. Was it politically correct as an Arab to harshly criticize the Arabs' study of Israel, with the continued Israeli denial of the Palestinians' inalienable right to self-determination? To be honest, I grappled with this question. Yet, my main concern was to highlight the importance of this topic to both Arab scholars and the Arab masses without manipulating their feelings. Arabs are known to be passionate about their feelings and dignity. It is not that the Arabs do not have talent. On the contrary, a quick look at academia reveals a number of amazing and world-class scholars whose contribution to the study of the Middle East is of great importance. But the fact remains that there have been objective conditions prevailing in the Arab world that make writing on Israel with detachment a difficult task to realize. Therefore, I contended that nothing short of exposing these conditions would help to change the status quo.

This study tackles an extremely important yet ignored topic: the underdevelopment of Israeli studies in the Arab world, and presents a critique of the status of Israeli studies in the Arab world. Evidently, substantial chunks of Israeli studies in the Arab world are weighed down by the domination of ideological epistemologies on scholarship. The situation is aggravated by the scholars' perception of their role as being to expose and delegitimize Israel, rather than to provide a sound knowledge of the other. Put differently, Israeli studies in the Arab world, for a variety of reasons, has never properly taken off. Hence, the main question of this intellectual inquiry addresses the impediments that prevented the development of Israeli studies in a more objective way.

Writing on Israel has taken the form of Israelism: a term that I coin for the sake of this study to refer to Arab scholars' style of writing on Israel. This style of writing is shaped by a set of ideas and misconceptions rooted in different ideologies and is one that is highly influenced by the perpetuation of the Arab–Israeli conflict. The outcome of Israelism is the failure to produce sound knowledge on Israel. Subordinating writing on Israel to the imperatives of the conflict has proved costly. Put simply, the conflict and ideologies should have less of a role in deciding the ontology and the epistemology of Israeli studies. The objective of the book is not only to provide a critique of the status of Israeli studies in the Arab world but also to argue that there should be an academic Arab perspective on how and what to study on Israel.

Given the sensitive nature of the Israeli topic among Arab scholars and media, I am aware of the possibility of accusations and labels waiting for me in the Arab world. However, I am ready and willing to face the criticism because my objective is to shake the foundations of the 'pseudo field' that has long been monopolized by certain scholars who claim absolute knowledge about the other. Yet, this will not change the fact that this kind of scholarship has to a great extent contributed to the weakness of the Arabs vis-à-vis Israel. Accusing and branding those who offer a new and controversial perspective will only negatively affect the Arabs' ability to understand and consequently respond to Israel.

The purpose of my book is not to condemn the Arabs, nor to underestimate the injustice imposed on the Palestinian people by Israel's continued denial of their right to self-determination. Writing a critique on this issue should be placed in its proper context and therefore should not take away a fraction of the Palestinians' rights to liberation and statehood. In writing this account, my intention is not to blame the ongoing violence on the Palestinians or the Israelis, as that question is beyond the scope of this inquiry. Nonetheless, I remain convinced that the Palestinian problem is the root cause of all the instabilities and authoritarianism in our region. Furthermore, I am unable to envisage peace and stability in the Middle East without first addressing this intractable conflict, which is, in my opinion, a key catalyst for all kinds of radicalism in the Middle East. This conflict has also been used as a tool in the hands of Arab regimes to deny their subjects true democracy and political freedom. That said, I strongly believe in the path of peaceful coexistence and historical reconciliation between the Arabs and the Israelis. Addressing and solving this conflict remains a prerequisite for achieving a long-lasting peace.

My purpose is to offer a constructive contribution towards laying the ground for better scholarship in the Arab world. The Arab world is full of talent, but the conflict has been so paramount that writing on Israel becomes a matter of struggle and strife rather than a means of exploration. By exposing the underpinning reasons behind the status of Israeli studies in the Arab world, I hope that the ensuing debate will serve to improve the state of the field. This book is overdue and I am pleased to have finally had the time to sit and write this modest contribution. In this context I would like to stress my conviction that the status of Israeli studies need not be static, it could be changed for the better. A change of the status quo is possible with the commitment of Arab academics and on the contingence of the emergence of a younger generation who will defy conformation to the current prevailing mode of writing. Nothing short of doing this will redeem Israeli studies in the Arab world.

The development of Israeli studies has been motivated by politics. Arab academics have sought mainly to gain influence within their societies and to mobilize the masses against Israel. Thus, Israeli studies were deemed as instrumental to this, not as a subject to be studied for its own sake. In this regard Edward Said's distinction between pure and political knowledge is important. Whereas Said argues that the Orient was studied in order to be dominated, this book makes the case that Israel was studied to be singled out as the main enemy that needed to be checked. The motivation is thus political. What is shocking about Arab specialists on Israel is their lack of the required skills for sound scholarly work. A handful of scholars are substituting indoctrination for scholarship.

The reason for the spread of this mode of writing on Israel was to help in the conduct of the Arab–Israeli conflict. For this reason, many scholars produced knowledge that was packaged to meet the needs of the ideological preferences of the Arab regimes and sometimes of the ideological oppositions. The result was distorted knowledge, with the goal of exposing Israel rather than attempting to understand the issue under study.

A range of political trends has emerged in the Arab world with regard to how to deal with Israel and the conflict. The first trend views the conflict as a zero-sum game: refusing to grant Israel a right to exist. This trend accepts the existence of Israel only as a fait accompli. Under no circumstances will Israel be dealt with lest this is seen as an aggression against Palestinian legitimate rights that are sacred and non-transferable. It sees Israel as a de facto force that has only the legitimacy of power that is derived from its organic link to Western states. Therefore, prudence is a must in this regard. The second trend, the liberal approach, focuses on Israel's membership to the UN and asserts that the Arabs cannot defeat it militarily. Those subscribing to this trend find it possible to accept Israel so long as it signs a comprehensive peace with the Arabs based on the 1967 borders. They believe a peace agreement will help contain Israel's expansionist tendencies. A third trend argues that Israel has no legitimacy whatsoever in Palestine and that it is not advisable to deal with it at all. Israel will never be a normal state and it is necessary to wait for a change in the balance of power in order to put an end to this country. A fourth trend is one adopted by Arab regimes. Each Arab regime adopts its own official discourse that constantly changes, and often clashes with that of other regimes. Their discourse has converged and diverged with the ideological currents (pan-Arabist and Islamic) according to the needs and leaning of a given regime. However, all of the Arab leaders have sought to use the conflict as a means to delay political reform, and to gain both internal and regional legitimacy. This is ironic because Israel was the main source of threat to these regimes.

Unfortunately, the outcome of all the above is that writing on Israel has become impressionistic or reactionary, angry or tense, or has simply been in line with the political atmosphere that has accompanied the peace process.

No agreement exists within these trends on the significance of studying Israel. It will suffice in this chapter to point out three opinions. The first opinion is apathetic toward the study of Israel and emphasizes the need to expose Israel's behavior and continually express anger at its policy. The second view calls for the understanding of Israel, not for the sake of pure knowledge, but rather for the need to 'know the enemy'. Here knowledge is instrumental in serving the ultimate goal: confronting Israel. The third and final view that I adopt in this study is the need to establish an Arab school dedicated to the study of Israel with the sole purpose of understanding Israel rather than in order to mobilize and fight. This view is what is lacking among the majority of Arab writers and academics.

Interestingly, the second and third views are not mutually exclusive. On the contrary they could complement each other. However, those who hold the second view will find themselves focusing on specific topics that will not ultimately lead to proper knowledge. The third and second views differ in scope. While the two views agree that the epistemology should be rooted in social sciences, their differences are concentrated on the ontological level. The goal should be to have sound and objective knowledge.

My research on published materials written up until the initiation of the peace process led me to the conclusion that the absence of well-qualified scholars is causing Arab scholarship to suffer. In fact, most of those who claimed expertise on Israel lacked basic yet indispensable skills, such as language competence and significant residency in Israel, and were therefore not equipped with the tools central to a sound analysis. One is rather struck by the sheer absence of Arab scholars who are able to handle the Hebrew language and thus overcome cultural barriers. This has been an enduring weakness in the field.

At this point, a brief history of the development of Israeli studies in the Arab world is in order. At the time of the establishment of Israel and the inception of the Arab–Israeli conflict, little had been written on Israel by Arab scholars. The few studies that did appear were meant to mobilize and present Israel as a fragile society that would collapse with the first bullet. These beliefs cost the Arabs dearly, and proved detrimental during intense times of war. One of the 1948 war participants confided in me their belief that Israel could be defeated with merely hundreds of good fighters.

To be fair, one should look at the intellectual and academic context of the early years of the conflict. Sound scholarly work and research in the Arab world was both poor and inaccurate, and there was little tradition of using social science tools in most Arab universities. Interestingly, much of the good writing on the region at that time was done by Western scholars and in English. Therefore, the underdevelopment of Israeli studies at that time was due to the state of Arab academia.

That said, the Six-Day War triggered a change in the Arab world. It sent a shock wave through a generation and triggered demands for an explanation of the defeat. It was obvious that the Arabs would stand to lose should this state of ignorance prevail. As Abdel Monem Said records, students of Cairo University who were to graduate and be recruited for the War of Attrition against Israel, demonstrated demanding that the university teach them about Israel. For the first time in 1970, Cairo University allowed the study of Israel's political system within the comparative government course.[1] Additionally, Egypt led the Arab world on this issue. In the aftermath of the war, the Center for

Palestinian and Zionist Studies was established by al-Ahram and in 1970 it was renamed as the Center for Political and Strategic Studies. The objective was to study Israeli and Palestinian societies. Also in 1968, the PLO established the Center for Palestinian Studies in Beirut, which published studies on the Arab–Israeli conflict and Israel. In 1977, Al-Jalil Center was established in Amman for the purpose of translating books written in Hebrew into Arabic. The Center has translated more than 100 books over the last 30 years. The Center of Arab Unity Studies was also established in Beirut in 1977. The Center for Political Research and Studies, part of Cairo University, was also established. The proliferation of centers indicated a marked difference in the attention given to Israel.

Academic work from this period suffered from problems such as the non-utilization of Israeli sources and the minimal implementation of field research. Ontologically, these studies only focused on elements that reinforced the Arabs' perception of Israel, and thus poorly contributed to the study of Israel's domestic politics. Hence this period did not give rise to a proper understanding of the importance of internal dynamics in Israel's foreign policy.

The attention to Israeli studies took a positive turn after the Oslo Agreement. Some centers opened in the West Bank and in Jordan. The Center for Strategic Studies (CSS) at the University of Jordan established an Israeli studies unit. It took the daring step of sending top students to study in Israel despite fierce criticism from many opposition groups strongly opposed to normalization with Israel.[2] However, the eruption of the second Intifada in September 2000 and the impasse in the peace process restricted the center's ability to recruit new scholars despite the CSS director's efforts to do so. The Palestinians meanwhile established a new center *Madar* (The Palestinian Center for Israeli Studies) to study Israeli politics and society. The center was established in 2000 and has been producing relatively well-researched material on Israel.

Objectives

Beyond unmasking the inherent bias in Arab scholars' study of Israel, this book exposes obstacles that have hindered the development of an understanding of Israel, such as inadequate scholarly communities in Arab universities and incompetent scholarship. Indeed, even today, few Arab universities run a teaching program on Israel. Despite the existence of some courses on Israel and the Arab–Israeli conflict, it was only very recently that Cairo University introduced a full program on Israeli studies. Moreover, even with the existence of good scholars who have sought, however belatedly, to correct the situation by equipping themselves with the basic skills of language competency and on-site residency, strong domestic opposition to any normalization of relations with Israel has prevented younger generations from traveling to Israel, thus failing to satisfy basic requirements for research.

A key objective of this intellectual inquiry is to set the historical, political and intellectual context that has propelled certain perspectives and discourses into hegemonic prominence. Needless to say this has greatly influenced the process of interpretation and understanding.

This book is both pioneering and timely. It calls for the establishment of an Arab school of thought for studying Israel based on the social sciences, which will utilize training mechanisms to equip younger generations of scholars with tools for objective knowledge. I strongly believe that developing a better and more vigorous scholarly project on Israel in the Arab world is a worthwhile undertaking. In fact, it is long overdue. The price of subordinating this crucial need to the imperatives of the conflict has cost the Arab world dearly and it is time that good scholars rose to the challenge. This book also attempts to identify the ideal conditions for developing the status of Israeli studies in the Arab world, and will hopefully stir a debate among experts on Israel in the Arab world, thus laying the ground for better scholarship in the region.

The importance of this book is threefold. Firstly, it aims to create awareness amongst Arab scholars that despite the abundance of books and articles on Israel, a sound accumulative understanding of Israel is absent. Secondly, the book has the potential to provoke a constructive debate concerning ways to overcome the impediments of developing Israeli studies in the Arab world. Finally, this book will potentially trigger the emergence of better, more thoroughly equipped scholars in the Arab world – certainly a progressive step regarding conflict resolution.

Given the critical nature of this inquiry, I am aware that many in the Arab world will be quick to attack this book, and describe it as 'playing into the hands of the enemy'. Those expected to voice their harshest criticism, are precisely the ones responsible for creating set boundaries of what and how to study Israel and the limits of acceptable conclusions. Any book that challenges their deep-seated ideological inclinations may be accused of being a mere Western tool, or abandoning the Palestinian cause, in an attempt to delegitimize the book and the author altogether.

These people are expected to dismiss the book while failing to present any counter-argument regarding the main issues it advances. Their main interest remains politically and ideologically motivated, which proves their alienation to scholarly work. Yet, the picture will not ultimately be gloomy. I am confident that there will be a number of Arab intellectuals who will do this book justice. I do not seek for them to concur with all of my statements or methodology, but I expect constructive criticism that will only enrich the topic under study. In other words, I hope that this book will jump-start a genuine dialogue and a debate over what went wrong and how to rectify the situation.

The Structure of the Book

The book is comprised of an introduction, four chapters and a conclusion. The introduction is a general tour of the evolvement of Israeli studies. Chapter One presents the conceptual framework of the book including the concept of area studies and how it has evolved. It sets the parameters of what constitutes area studies and also touches on the controversy of area studies and social science disciplines and answers the basic question of whether Israeli studies in the Arab world can qualify as area studies. Chapter One also pays substantial attention to the underlying reasons behind the underdevelopment of Israeli studies in the Arab world. Chapter Two examines the pan-Arabist and leftist discourses and how they delineate the boundaries of knowledge on Israel. Similarly, Chapter Three examines the Islamic discourse and its impact on Israeli studies. Chapter Four examines the role of Arab regime's discourse and how the conflict was used to manipulate internal politics in some Arab countries to permit the survival of regimes. The conclusion presents the main findings with particular emphasis on proposing mechanisms to equip younger scholars in the Arab world with different methodologies and perspectives to generate a more comprehensive knowledge of Israel.

Notes

—　—

1　Abdel Monem Said, *al-Ahram al-Iqtisadi* (*Economic Ahram*), 23 January 2003.
2　For a discussion of the controversy of normalization, see Hassan A. Barari, *Jordan and Israel: Ten Years Later* (Amman: CSS, 2004).

1

Conceptual Framework

——

Scholarly interpretation is never neutral or objective, it is always linked to certain theoretical and methodological perspectives that determine the course of understanding and interpretation.

Hisham Sharabi
Theory, Politics and the Arab World: Critical Responses

Introduction

This book addresses an overlooked, yet important phenomenon: the underdevelopment of Israeli studies in the Arab world, particularly during the first three decades of the conflict. It presents a critical assessment of the status of Israeli studies since the establishment of Israel in 1948. Its main thesis is that despite the existence of a plethora of books and academic articles on Israel written in Arabic, Arab scholars have failed to produce sound, objective knowledge on Israel. Israeli studies in the Arab world are weighed down by biased projection, ideological deformation, predisposition and the need to expose rather than to understand or explain the 'other'. Arab scholars' writing on Israel has, to a great extent, been informed by the persistence of the Arab–Israeli conflict, a conflict that accentuates the role of ideologies in Israeli studies. The prolongation of the conflict has instilled a closed belief system in Arab scholarship that has not brought about sound insights into Israeli studies. In effect, academic writing, despite some slight improvements in the last decade, is more of a tool of resistance against Israel than a mechanism for understanding.

This book answers two interrelated basic questions. Firstly, has Israeli studies developed in the Arab world as a field of area studies? If the answer is yes, why have most Arab scholars failed to produce sound knowledge on Israel? In other words, the book is an attempt to deconstruct the dominant discourses on Israel through an in-depth examination of the forces at play.

Until recently, there has been no debate in the Arab world on how to study Israel. Arab researchers on the whole are prone to believe that it is not possible to understand Israel without understanding Zionism. Yet every country has its own quirks and should not be placed outside the confines of scholarly and academic research. Thus, the prevailing Arab perspective, which focuses on Zionism as the key independent variable, is not completely correct. Despite the importance of understanding Zionism, I argue that Israel can be studied by utilizing the well-known epistemologies in social sciences.

Notwithstanding the recent emergence of some centers and programs devoted to studying Israel, there have been few serious attempts on the part of Arab scholars to critically assess Arab scholarship on Israel. However, there have been three belated, yet significant, attempts to assess Israeli studies. Perhaps the first study that called for the need to begin studying Israeli society and politics, came ironically from two prominent Arab–Israeli scholars: Azmi Bishara (a member of the Israeli Knesset who has chosen to live in exile) and Adel Manna (an Arab–Israeli historian) who co-edited a book published in 1995. In the book's introduction, the authors make the case that the weakness of Israeli studies in the Arab world is due to the tendency to overlook Israel's internal issues. The book's main drawback is that it does not make an in-depth attempt to allude to the wider picture that underpins the situation that led to the failure of Israeli studies.[1]

A second attempt was a workshop I organized at the Center for Strategic Studies (CSS) at the University of Jordan in Amman in October 2002. The aim of the workshop was to build on the above-mentioned book and discuss the underlying reasons for the paucity of sound Arab scholarship on Israel. I invited top Arab experts on Israel. Although there was no agreement among participants on the reasons for the weakness of Israeli studies, the discussion was both enlightening and productive. It is my hope to organize a follow-up workshop on the same theme, if funding permits, to enable me to continue to create awareness among the epistemic community of the need to embark on a new way of studying Israel.

A third attempt took place when the Center for Political Research and Studies in Cairo organized a major conference in December 2002 entitled "Israel from Within". The proceedings of the conference were published in two volumes.[2] Explicit in the papers presented and the final report was the conviction that Arab scholars have produced good knowledge on Israel and its foreign policy. In fact, the main question and theme of the conference was: what has been achieved after four decades of studying Israel? And how should this knowledge and increased understanding of Israel be employed? Implicit in the final report was the idea that knowledge on Israel is not gathered just for sake of knowledge, but rather is linked to Arab security and existence. Despite the importance of the conference, it did not ask the right question: what has gone wrong with Israeli studies in the Arab world? While the three attempts indicate that there is at least readiness to critically discuss the status of Israeli studies, none have focused thoroughly and meticulously on the obstacles that have impeded the development of sound knowledge on Israel. This book fills this gap.

The Issue of Perspective

Edward Said's *Orientalism* presents a harsh critique of Middle Eastern studies in the West. He makes the case that the relationship between the Orient and the Occident is one of power and domination. He exposes and characterizes Western scholarship on the Middle East as being a style of "domination, restructuring, and having authority over the Orient".[3] Said raises an important question that is relevant to my study: is it possible to have non-political scholarship? Similarly, Hisham Sharabi asks "Can knowledge be objective when it is on the other".[4] Sharabi answers this question in an indirect yet subtle way. In his seminal book, *Theory, Politics and the Arab World*, Sharabi argues that academic writing cannot be objective. He puts it succinctly: "Scholarly interpretation is never neutral or objective, it is always linked to certain theoretical and methodological perspectives that determine the course of understanding and interpretation."[5] Leonard Binder echoes Sharabi's argument when he writes that area studies is political.[6] The link between perspective and interpretation certainly applies in the assessment of Israeli studies. While a perspective constitutes one way of assessing the relationship, it also presents serious constraints. Examining these constraints is important in order to determine their affect on our understanding.

It is important to see how a certain perspective can become a hegemonic discourse. Some aspects of Antonio Gramsci's concept of hegemony are of paramount importance to the understanding of the predominance of certain perspectives. Cultural hegemony in this sense is crucial for a proper understanding of the reasons behind the production of certain knowledge. Gramsci's ideas were based on Marx's notion of "false consciousness" which refers to a state in which people are ideologically blinded by the domination they experience. Yet, unlike Marx, who views society as a structure in which the economy is the base for a political superstructure, Gramsci draws our attention to the paramount importance of ideas and symbols to the ruling ideology. Hegemony is a process whereby the dominant class, via access to social institutions such as the media, promulgate values and ideas, and fortify their control. The role of the media, according to Gramsci, is not to watch the government, but to shore up the world view of the ruling class. Gramsci's concept of the media is indeed relevant to the interwar period (1919–39) and continues to be relevant in much of the Arab world. Here the media's role, for an extended period of time, has been to propagate the ideas and values of the ruling elite as well as advance the dominant ideologies and perspectives. Simply put, the media has contributed enormously to the process of mystification that has plagued much of Arab understanding of Israel.

Dominant perspectives are closely linked to collective and, on many occasions, an individual's closed belief systems. Beliefs are a set of ideas that writers believe in without being able to verify.[7] Such belief systems (whether collective or individual) condition much interpretation and analysis. Indeed, writers with a closed belief system (most ideological writers fit this definition) will find it hard to accept any new information that does not fit within their set of ideas and beliefs. Critical social theory indicates that we can assign an explanatory power to the belief system. The reason for this assertion, and my agreement with the critical social theory, is that knowledge of social events is not one and the same as science. Science is useful in understanding the natural world. On this particular theme, two points need to be considered. Firstly, social reality does not present itself as something that is both external and objective. Secondly, scholars unknowingly or unconsciously play a key role in constructing the social reality under discussion.

When it comes to Israel, the hegemony of certain perspectives and belief systems is evident. It is reinforced by a socialization process from the family, religion, schools and the media and accentuated by the domination of ethnocentrism in analysis and research.[8] Throughout this book, the term 'Israelism' will be used to refer to the mode and style of writing that Arab writers use whenever Israel is the topic and Israelists to refer to the writers themselves. The style is driven by a perceived set of ideas rooted in ideology that subordinates pure knowledge to the imperatives of the Arab–Israeli conflict, and an obsession with the absolute justice of the Palestinian cause.

One can think of specific tenets of the hegemonic ideologies and perspectives on Israel. In this regard, Israelism is clustered around a combination of convictions, assumptions and timeless facts. Firstly, there is the political, and perhaps ideological, illusion that Israel will eventually disappear – the inevitability syndrome (see p. 10 below). Secondly, Israel is understood as an advanced outpost of imperialism with a role to serve Western powers. Thirdly, there is the sense that domestic politics in Israel is nothing but a smokescreen for Israel's functional role of serving the imperial interests in the region. In other words, the internal political dynamics within Israel are a kind of play where parties are assigned different roles. Fourthly, is the idea that Israel's resilience in the region is only due to Western support. Explicit in this notion is the idea that once the West adopts a 'hands-off' policy, Israel's eventual defeat will start. Finally, there is the idea that Israel is a unique state that should be studied with reference to Zionism, lending little value to the discipline of social science when it comes to understanding Israel.

Like all area studies, Israeli studies in the Arab world have, by and large, served political ends.[9] In fact, area studies as a concept came about during the Second World War, when American leaders realized that there was a need for language and history experts to supply them with knowledge on other cultures. It was within this context of global competition that area studies emerged. Seen from this perspective, knowledge of the other is meant to realize hegemony and domination, confirming the importance of Edward Said's distinction between pure and political knowledge.[10]

Area studies assumes that cultural differences are important for understanding any topic under study. Writing without taking into account the uniqueness of the region or the state under study is likely to lead to distorted knowledge. Although area studies offers enormous knowledge, it is often criticized for being obsessed with details at the expense of more simple assumptions, as well as for lacking conceptual sophistication or methodological rigor. The debate regarding the utility of area studies is known as the area studies controversy.[11] According to Bahgat Korany, although much of the criticism against areas studies in the 1950s was warranted, these critiques are perceived as outdated ideas of international relations today. Korany rightly argues against dichotomies in scholarly knowledge, advocating instead the integration of the two perspectives (area studies and social sciences). Area study specialists should carry on working within the "traditions of established disciplines".[12] Put differently, area study experts should be discipline-oriented scholars. To a considerable extent, this is what is lacking in the Arab world regarding Israeli studies.

Additionally, Leonard Binder rightly points to a flaw in area studies by critically questioning whether area studies can act as a tool to further our understanding of the topic under inquiry or "whether they determine what can be known".[13] Of course, the former confirms that we are on the right track and that we are positive about our conclusions on the topic of study. The latter means that area studies merely validate general ideas. Scholars who practice area studies and who are discipline-oriented are closer to the first case. However, some experts rebuff the utility of disciplines altogether.

Interestingly, global developments that have unfolded in the last decade, such as the end of the Cold War and technological advancements in communication, coupled with the spread of globalization, have led to the emergence of some who question the validity or utility of area studies. The argument is that "it is no longer important for Western scholars to acquire detailed information about the history, culture or languages of most developing countries".[14] The same could be applied to some Arab scholars who see Israel within this context. Some experts on Israel, with no linguistic background in Hebrew, make the case that knowledge of Hebrew is not necessary to study Israel thoroughly.

Edward Said's distinction between pure and political knowledge is thus very appropriate. Whereas Said argues that the Orient was studied in order to be dominated, this book makes the case that Israel is studied to single it out as the main enemy that needs to be checked at every step.

Arab Scholarship: The Underdevelopment of the Field

Evidently, the need for Arab scholars' writing on Israel stems not only from the perceived lack of knowledge on Israeli politics, but also from the need to bolster the Arab side in the ongoing conflict. For these reasons, many scholars produced knowledge that was packaged to meet the ideological preferences of the regimes and sometimes of the opposition. This produced distorted knowledge rather than a more sensitive and creative understanding of the issues under study, thus causing indoctrination to replace scholarship.

Of all the setbacks that plague Israeli studies in the Arab world, the indifference to Israeli domestic politics and society remains a serious long-term problem. It is my conviction that short of unpacking the black box, to use the parlance of Realism, no proper knowledge on Israel is possible. Since Arab academics belittle the importance of internal dynamics in Israel, there have been no serious academic efforts to unpack Israel in order to understand its intricacies. One is rather struck by the modest amount of written material on Israel in the first two decades after its establishment. This is even more perplexing when one compares the number of studies that appeared in Israel on several Arab countries. This is not to say that Arab studies in Israel are objective, but the case remains that an Israeli school of thought has emerged to determine how to handle the Arab region.

Israeli studies in the Arab world have been built on two assumptions[15] that negatively impacted the epistemology and the ontology of Israeli studies in the Arab world. The first was that Israel was nothing but an artificial entity and a passing phenomenon and therefore it was neither advisable nor necessary to study Israel from within. The second assumption was derived from the ideological and political illusion that Israel will disappear over time. This is what can be called the 'inevitability syndrome'. For example, in his book on Zionism, Khalid Qashteini argues that "perhaps the most importance conclusion of this book leads us to rule out the probability of peaceful coexistence between the Arab entity and the Zionist one and to lean toward the vanishing of the Zionist entity as a final chapter of the tragedy of the long conflict".[16] This 'inevitability' mindset also led to the conclusion that there was no need to study Israel from within. According to this line of thinking, an observation of Israel's actions in the region is sufficient to understand Israel. Unfortunately, much of this writing has come under the rubric of timeless convictions rather than knowledge.

Coupled with this assumption was the deep-rooted ideological conviction that Israel lacked legitimacy and the conditions to sustain its existence. This view maintained that the main constitutive components of Israel are its foreign policy and its role in the region. The role is as an outpost for Western imperialism, and is determined by the need to serve Western powers. This assumption has marred the work of well-known scholars, such as Nasr Shamali, and critically prejudiced their findings. For example, Shamali takes issue with the idea that knowledge of domestic politics is important for understanding Israel's action in the region. Even a political turnabout such as the Likud victory in 1977, was not seen as important and could not be understood as independent of Israel's role in serving imperialism. Political parties, according to this line of thinking, existed not as a reflection of socio-economic or political and religious reality, but only to respond to imperialist objectives. Bluntly put, the internal dynamic is a direct function of external demands rather than a function of the socio-economic reality of Israeli society. According to Shamali, the parties' main task is to create a conducive social and political atmosphere, capable of placing Israelis in a suitable position to serve the global system. The Jews, according to him, were assembled and dispatched to

Palestine for this purpose. Explicit in his thesis is the conviction that the purpose of political parties is to control the discrepancies within Israeli society in order to continue serving imperialist interests in the region.[17] Let it suffice to say here that this trend in analysis is both erroneous and an ideological oversimplification of a very complicated reality.

Ultimately, the above two assumptions proved to be grossly wrong. Some prominent scholars like Abdelwahab Elmessiri (who dedicated volumes of books to Zionism and Judaism) fell into this simplistic ideological trap. Such scholars could not free themselves from the illusion of Israel's inevitable vanishing and its functional role to serve the West and its imperialist agenda.[18] Although most of Elmessiri's writings were well researched and fully documented (more on this point later in the book), they claim *a priori* that Israel has a functional role to emasculate the Arab countries and to serve Western and imperialist interests in the region, without balancing that carefully with Israel's independent role as an actor in international politics.

A key problem that has dominated the Arab mindset for decades is the inability to make a distinction between the perception of the lack of legitimacy of Israel and the legitimacy of Israel as a topic to be studied. Thus, writing on Israel, particularly in the press, has become a means to struggle or fight against Israel and mobilize the masses, rather than a means of explaining and understanding the country. Indeed, the objective has been to delegitimize Israel, leaving academic writing on Israel to be seen as conferring legitimacy to an otherwise 'illegitimate' entity.

Until 1967, there were no worthy studies on Israel in the Arab world. A leading Arab scholar, Abdel Monem

Said, has criticized that period for ignoring the study of Israel at a time when knowledge of the other was vitally important. He argued: "despite the magnitude of the conflict and the description of the conflict as a zero-sum game, studying Israel was not favorable. It was seen as a kind of pan-national filthiness as studying Israel meant somehow the acknowledgement of a fraudulent entity."[19] Israel was projected as an 'illegitimate' state with a fragile society that would not be able to survive a military confrontation with the Arabs. Interestingly, justifying the conflict with Israel not only entailed offering proof for Israel's lack of legitimacy, but also proof of its weakness. For this reason, and as I will discuss later in this book, Islamist writings provide a portrayal of brave and heroic Muslims as in opposition to the 'gutlessness' of the Jews. Since the statements are wrapped in apocalyptic language, they are taken by the masses as a given truth. For instance, in a victory speech given by Hassan Nasserallah in the aftermath of the unilateral Israeli withdrawal from southern Lebanon in 2000, Nasserallah explicitly states that Israel is weaker than a spider web and is bound to collapse soon.[20] Though the spider web looks solid in appearance, it disintegrates easily as it is wiped away. The reason for the comparison is to persuade people of the weakness of the Israeli state and encourage an Arab revolt to bring about Israel's collapse.

Interestingly, Israelis often reiterate this metaphor to protect Israel's image, and justify their aggression. And this thinking influenced Israel's blunder in conducting the Lebanon war of July 2006. However, the prevalence of such discourse led to an Arab underestimation of Israel in 1948 and 1967, not to mention during the second Intifada and its militarization. Yet, this kind of discourse cannot account for the resilience of Israel. On many occasions, Arab scholars invoke the West and its support for Israel to account for the latter's triumphs and to galvanize the masses. It has become axiomatic of pan-Arab nationalist writers to blame Israel's success on the external factor. To them, the weakness of Israel and the key role external support plays in Israel's survival are both proven facts.

Much has been said and written about conspiratorial thinking against the interests of the Islamic and Arab nations. This reflects a mindset that has plagued some of the otherwise good writings on Israel. The belief that there has been an international conspiracy against the Arab and Muslim worlds with Israel at the center is a key impediment that has prevented scholars from seeing reality. This mindset ignores the role of socio-economic factors in determining the conduct of people and states. More troubling is the scholars' inability to look deep into the conflict and see the problems of the side they belong to. This leads people to see themselves as victims, with no power to change the situation. Conspiracy theories, according to some scholars "encourage victimization, powerlessness, and pessimism".[21]

The most salient trend in studying Israel remains, in essence, an ideological one that suffers greatly from a deficit in epistemologies. This has indeed hindered the development of a serious study of Israel in the Arab world. Academic scholarship remains hostage to ideology and the persistence of the conflict. For this reason, much of the writings emerge within the context of adopting a particular political stand and justifying that ideologically. The resultant text is one that is inaccurate and focused on description rather than explanation. Much more troubling is that this trend presents events as though they are static, which leads to myths rather than knowledge. These ideological writers suffer from the fact that they have a closed belief system that tends to discard any new information that does not conform to their beliefs. Three ideological currents have produced dominant discourses. The pan-Arabist, the Marxist and the Islamic discourses have provided the overriding framework that conditions much of the understanding and interpretation of Israel. Indeed, the three discourses have engulfed the masses and defined the boundaries of how and what to study. For the first two decades of the conflict with Israel, Arab scholars overemphasized the link between Israel (Zionism) and the imperial powers in the region. The obsession with this kind of thinking produced the two above-mentioned flawed assumptions that led to Arab scholars' indifference to the study of Israel from within. The perpetuation of the Arab–Israeli conflict only accentuated the role of ideology in the process of understanding and interpretation.

Reductionist analysis is also one of the causes of the modest achievement of Arab scholarship on Israel. After all, some writers employed only one variable to explain major events. One example of this would be when a writer accounts for the outbreak of the Six-Day War as being Israel's need to find a solution to its chronic economic problems. Another example is shown by writers' attempts to explain why Israel opted for a peaceful settlement. The answer provided to this question is that Israel has replaced deterrence (a crucial concept in the Israeli security approach) with peace theory, which is based on trading land for peace.[22] Both explanations are erroneous because they downplay the weight of other far more important factors i.e. strategic consideration and the balance of power rationale.

Also, area specialists often reiterate the mantra that basic precepts such as Zionism and expansionism are the root cause of Israeli policies. These concepts are understood to have a timeless impact on Israel. It does not matter which particular area specialists are studying, be it the economy, sociology or the politics of Israel, the origin is always Zionism and the Zionists' scheme to expand at the expense of Arab land. Although I concur that there is an element of truth in this assumption, I argue that Israel is far more complex than that.

That said, it would not be possible to account for the underdevelopment of Israeli studies without placing this in a wider perspective. A lack of academic freedom and political freedom has had enormous impact on the status and quality of social sciences in the Arab world. There are many topics that are considered culturally or politically taboo. For this reason, tolerance of other 'radical' views has proved to be difficult to sustain in the Arab world. The absence of political freedom is well documented and is related to the spread and survival of different authoritarian Arab regimes. Likewise, Arab academia is also subordinated to the imperative of the political atmosphere. In many places in the Arab world, it is difficult to take an independent academic choice without being questioned by universities and research centers. In 2007, a prominent Jordanian scholar was fired from his job at a research center at one of the Jordanian universities simply because he wrote a paper (against his boss's political opinion) for an American think tank that was seen by his boss as being a 'Zionist' institution in Washington, DC. Firing someone from a university because he holds different political views and because he has upheld his right to make academic choices, is simply a blatant testimony of the lack of academic freedom. There are certainly other cases where people have paid dearly for their insistence on their academic freedom, but the overwhelming majority usually comply with one of the dominant discourses.

Finally, Arab scholars have failed to match their Israeli counterparts in challenging the official and ideological narrative of their own states as the Israeli 'New Historians' did in Israel. While I believe in the Palestinians' just cause for liberation and self-determination, I argue for the need for a revisionist Arab school of thought. It is striking how the interpretations of the New Historians were used in the Arab world as further proof of their righteous and factual positions. The absence of this school of thought has ultimately to do with the regimes themselves.

I would, however, like to point to the fact that the above-mentioned impediments have not precluded a few scholars from producing sound knowledge. For example, an excellent book, from a well-known Palestinian professor, Khalil Shikaki, appeared in the middle of the second Intifada (more on this point later in the following chapters).

Notes

——

1   Adel Manna and Azmi Bishara (eds.), *Dirasat fil Mujtama' Al-israeli* (Studies on Israeli Society) (Israel: Center for Arab Society in Israel, 1995).

2   Nadia Mamoud Mustafa and Hiba Ra'ouf Ezzat (eds.), *Israel min eldakhil* (Israel from Within) (Cairo: Center for Political Research and Studies, 2003).

3   Edward Said, *Orientalism: Western Conceptions of the Orient* (England: Penguin Books, 1979), p. 3.

4   Hisham Sharabi (ed.), *Theory, Politics and the Arab World: Critical Responses* (New York and London: Routledge, 1990), p. 2.

5   *Ibid.*, p. 1.

6   Leonard Binder, "Area Studies: A Critical Reassessment", in Leonard Binder (ed.), *The Study of the Middle East: Research and Scholarship in the Humanities and the Social Sciences* (New York: John Wiley and Sons, 1976), pp. 1–28.

7   John Maclean, "Belief Systems and Ideology in International Relations: A Critical Approach", in Richard Little and Steve Smith (eds.), *Belief System and International Relations* (Oxford: Basil Blackwell Ltd, 1988), p. 67.

8   Ken Booth, *Strategy and Ethnocentrism* (London: Croom Helm, 1979), p. 15.

9   For further details on the emergence of area studies see Leonard Binder, *The Study of the Middle East.*

10   Edward Said, *Orientalism: Western Conceptions of the Orient.*

11   See Mark Tessler (ed.), *Area Studies and Social Science: Strategies for Understanding Middle East Politics* (Bloomington & Indianapolis: Indiana University Press, 1999).

12   Bahgat Korany, "International Relations Theory: Contributions for Research in the Middle East", in Mark Tessler (ed.), *Area Studies and Social Science: Strategies for Understanding Middle East Politics*

(Bloomington & Indianapolis: Indiana University Press, 1999), pp. 148–49.

13   Leonard Binder, *The Study of the Middle East*, p. 15.

14   Mark Tessler, *Area Studies and Social Science*, p. xi.

15   Adel Manna and Azmi Bishara (eds.), *Dirasat fil Mujtama' Al-israeli* (Studies on Israeli Society), p. 8.

16   Kahlid Qashteini, *Takween Asahyuniyah* (The Making of Zionism) (Beirut: Al-Mu'asasah Al-Arabiya Lidirasat wal Nashr, 1986).

17   Nasr Shamali and Hisham Al-Dajani, *Al-Ahzab wal Kutal Asiyasyyah fi Israel* (Political Parties and Blocs in Israel) (Beirut: Maktab El-Khadamat Atiba'yah, 1986).

18   Interview with Abdelwahab Elmessiri, www.arabiyat.com (Accessed 2 November 2006).

19   Abdel Monem Said, *al-Ahram al-Iqtisadi* (*Economic Ahram*), 23 January 2003.

20   His speech is known widely as 'the spider-web speech'.

21   Anita M. Waters, "Conspiracy Theories as Ethno-sociologies: Explanation and Intention in African American Political Culture", *Journal of Black Studies*, vol. 28, no. 1 (September, 1997), p. 113.

22   Mahmoud Amin Ataya, *Al-Nizam Sharq Awsati Al-Jadid: Al-Mukhatatat Al-Israeliya Lilhaymanah Ala Elmantiqa Al-Arabiya* (Middle Eastern Order: Israeli Schemes for Hegemony Over the Arab Area) (Beirut: Al-Manara, 1995).

2

Pan-Arabist and Leftist Discourses

— —

In Palestine, the imperialists and Zionists collaborated to evict our people from their land. They said and they are still saying that "Israel" has come to stay. But the Arab people retorts, in Palestine, Egypt, Syria and in every other Arab country, and the disaster is ten years old, that "Israel" has come to go away and with it imperialism will go too.

Michel Aflaq, June 7, 1957

Introduction

Central to this chapter is the assumption that due to the compelling supremacy of pan-Arabist and Leftist discourses during the first two decades of the conflict, studying Israel from within was ignored or at best relegated. Another main objective in this chapter is to establish the link between the perspective (ideological discourse) and interpretation of the study (Israel and Zionism). The vigorous intellectual discourses of both currents have electrified the masses and set the political agenda of the region as a whole. The hegemonic discourse was, by and large, pan-Arabism. It is this, to use the Gramscian parlance, hegemonic discourse that has conditioned much of the epistemology and the ontology of the study of Israel. It deserves attention given the ascendance to power of a handful of powerful pan-Arabists such as Nasser and the Ba'ath parties in both Syria and Iraq.

Unsurprisingly, there was barely a book written in Arabic on Israel during this period that did not focus on the organic link between Zionism and imperialism. According to these discourses, Israel's foreign policy vis-à-vis the region was the most salient component of Israel, which was in turn determined by the imperial interests in the region. Indeed, the persistence of the Arab–Israeli conflict, and its ostensibly irreconcilable nature, created an intellectual atmosphere in which these two discourses thrived. Hence, scholars became susceptible to their compelling power.

Whilst pan-Arab nationalism and Marxist ideologies were by no means identical, I have brought their respective discourses together into one chapter as they had much in common regarding the link between Zionism and imperialism that warrants dealing with them together. Seen in this way, the bifurcation of views between the two discourses became gradually irrelevant as Nasser of Egypt gained regional prominence in the aftermath of his successful revolution in 1952 and the departure of British forces from Egypt. Against this backdrop, Marxists, particularly after the changing image and role of Zionism and what seemed to be the unstoppable tide of pan-Arabism, began to lean towards the pan-Arabist discourse. From the Marxist movements' vantage point, there was a need to reposition themselves within the national struggle against imperialism.[1] This chapter provides the historical context for the ascendance of the pan-Arabist and Marxist discourses in the Arab world and how that impacted the way Israel and Zionism were projected. The chapter clarifies the main analytical concepts that guide the pan-Arabist understanding of Israel. It also presents some writing examples.

The Historical Context

The Ascendance of Pan-Arabism

Historically speaking, Arab nationalism (henceforth referred to as pan-Arabism) predated the establishment of the state of Israel and the advent of the Jewish–Arab struggle for Palestine. Its inception came as a reaction to external factors. In effect, the very idea of nationalism was a European invention. Most accounts of the beginning of pan-Arabism indicate that its sentiments came to the fore just before the eclipse of the Ottoman Empire, under which the Arabs were at best docile and complacent. The dismemberment of the Ottoman Empire coupled with the Great Arab Revolt of 1916 accentuated Arab ambitions for independence and unity. Yet, to their vexation, the Arabs realized neither independence nor unity. They were denied the right to self-determination by the imperial powers of the time and were subsequently colonized, with North Africa and Egypt falling under the rule of the European colonial powers during the eighteenth and nineteenth centuries.

The creation of the Middle Eastern state system, including the Arab states, was determined, to a great extent, by the external colonial powers. From the vantage point of the indigenous Arabs, the resultant Arab states were, to say the least, artificial which led to further fragmentation and divisions. It was not unnatural, therefore, that some intellectuals spearheaded a meticulous intellectual effort to bring about the unification of the 'Arab nation', a nation which remained divided and fragmented. Against this background, the call for unity constituted a major tenet on the part of many intellectuals and politicians alike. Perhaps the most important figure among Arab intellectuals was Sati al-Husri who took it upon himself to promote the idea of Arabism and nationalism. Al-Husri was born in Yemen, studied in Turkey and spoke French and Turkish. In fact, according to some accounts he spoke Arabic with a slight Turkish accent. Nevertheless, the impact of his writings was immense among people who hitherto had never experienced the idea of nationalism. The main focus of al-Husri and his contemporary nationalist generation was to highlight to the public the importance of having one state based on what they deemed as one Arab nation. Influenced by the concept of cultural nationalism professed by the German Johann Gottfried Herder, al-Husri stressed the importance of the organic and symbiotic relationship between nationalism and language.[2] To al-Husri, the people who spoke one language, i.e. the Arabs, have "one heart and a common soul. As such, they constitute one nation, therefore they are entitled to have one amalgamated state."[3]

Conspicuously, the spread of pan-Arabism did not take place overnight. Despite the Arab sentiments, the ideology of pan-Arabism remained confined but not limited to a small numbers of Arab Christian intellectuals who found in nationalism, rather than religion, a better framework to achieve equality in the nevertheless predominantly Muslim societies. Despite the Ottomans' defeat, and their ultimate retreat from the Arab region, the Arabs were not granted independence. The advent of colonial powers, the emergence of Zionism and the influence of modernization came to define much of pan-Arabist ideology. This process of modernization required the molding of Arab societies along the lines of Western ones, a process that entailed building a secular educational system in which secular and Western ideas were injected.

Put simply, the emergence of pan-Arabism was triggered mainly by external factors. However, what catapulted this ideology into prominence and relevance, and lent it some credibility – the crux of the matter – was an internal dynamic within a major Arab country: Egypt. Nasser's revolution of 1952 marked a new chapter in Arab history. Interestingly, Nasser's revolution had much more to do with a desire to get rid of the British presence in the Suez Canal than with Egypt's humiliating defeat at the hands of the Zionists. But Nasser and his regime led the Arab nation in a struggle against colonialism, imperialism and Zionism. It is worth pointing out, however, that despite the rhetoric of pan-Arabism, the unity priority was never shared by all countries (more on this in Chapter Four).

Pan-Arabism's view of the Palestinian–Israeli conflict is not one of two national movements each claiming the same land. Rather, it sees it as a conflict between an Arab national movement and a religious community that has no right to self-determination. To pan-Arabists, Jews do not constitute a nation. Therefore, the conflict is with Zionism as a Western phenomenon that is akin to, though not identical to, imperialism and colonialism. For this reason, parallels drawn between Zionism and the French settler community in Algeria are central to pan-Arabist discourse on this issue. For Islamists, the analogy is with the crusaders' 200-year occupation of Palestine. A key attribute of this discourse is that Zionism, and by extension Israel is going to vanish. This is the inevitability syndrome that characterizes both the Pan-Arabist and Marxist Leftist discourse, and the Islamist discourse.

The Arab Marxist Left

Paradoxically, and despite the universal aspect of Marxism and the presence of numerous Marxist-based parties and movements in the Arab world, little effort was made to unite them into one movement. Marxist parties experienced different conditions according to the country in which they were operating. This section is not a chronology of the development of Marxist parties, but rather is intended to set the historical and intellectual context of the way this trend, on the whole, viewed Zionism and Israel. For this reason, I will not touch on the internal divisions of each Marxist group in each individual country.

The position of the Arab Marxist Left prior to, and after the establishment of, the state of Israel was highly informed by the position of the Soviet Union and the international communist movement. Zionism, during the British mandate of Palestine, was seen in negative terms. Joel Beinin analyzes the Egyptian Marxist groups and how they viewed Zionism. In his words, Zionism was looked upon as a

> Settler-colonial movement expropriating the rights of the indigenous population in alliance with British Imperialism.

> Before October 1947, communists had argued that creating a
> Jewish state would permanently exacerbate relations between
> Jews and Arabs and provide the Western imperial powers with
> an excuse to continue to intervene in regional affairs.[4]

Even some Jewish Marxist factions, such as *Hashomer hatza'ir* (an Israeli political party), regarded the establishment of a pure Jewish state as an injustice to the Palestinian majority, and it therefore advocated a bi-national state.[5] However, the position of Israeli Marxists is beyond the scope of this section and this book.

Driven by its anti-imperialist leanings, it was not unnatural that the Soviet Union advocated positions advancing an anti-imperialist struggle in order to bring about an eventual expulsion of Britain from the Middle East. This objective conditioned the Soviet Union's attitude towards the partition of Palestine in 1947. Zionism was seen, for a brief period, as a powerful anti-imperialist force. Arab Marxists' acceptance of this reasoning led them to belittle the nationalist and ethnic nature of Zionism. The redefinition of Zionism as part of an anti-imperial front downplayed the national Jewish nature of the movement for years to come. Their vision was influenced by the "linear and teleological Marxism and Comintern, which regarded anti-imperialist national liberation movements as inevitably allied to the progress of international socialism".[6] Communists therefore made a distinction between their support for the creation of Israel, and their opposition to Zionism.

On the whole, Arab Marxists saw in the partition a mechanism to force the British from the region and achieve independence. Naively, they thought this partition would lead to a united Palestine. After the guns were silenced in 1949, Marxists continued to advocate a peaceful settlement to the Arab–Israeli conflict. Marxists were not ideologically against peace with Israel, but they argued that it was impossible to have peace with Israel until it disentangled itself from imperialism. This position was mainly taken by Syrian Marxists and was then adopted by Egyptian Marxists who also advocated the installment of elected Arab governments to bring about peace in the Middle East.

The emergence of Nasser as an anti-imperialist, pan-Arab leader transformed the political environment in which the Marxists operated. Evidently, the second half of the 1950s was a revolutionary period in inter-Arab politics. Nasser emerged from the Bandung Non-Aligned Conference in 1955 as a leading anti-imperialist leader. Nasser managed to conclude a Czech arms deal, which boosted his standing among the Arabs. The subsequent nationalization of the Suez Canal and Nasser's political victory over Israel, France and Britain combined, in 1956, to catapult Nasser to an undisputedly high status among the Arab masses. To the chagrin of Marxists, they were forced to assess their stand vis-à-vis Nasser and eventually gave in to his leadership.

The demise of the European colonial powers (Britain and France) in the Middle East, and the strategic vacuum this created, was an invitation to the new superpowers to fill the vacuum. The Soviet Union was quick to capitalize on this unprecedented opportunity and saw Nasser as a potential ally. The close interaction between pan-Arabism and Marxism was given impetus by the imperatives of the Cold War and the rapprochement between Nasser and the Eastern bloc under the leadership of the Soviet Union. Nasser used the global rivalry between the two superpowers, the United States and the USSR, to play one off against the other in order to further his interests. The announcement of the Eisenhower Doctrine in January 1957 was perceived as an American attempt to contain Nasser's growing influence in the Arab world. American policy in the region, particularly in Lebanon and Jordan, only confirmed Nasser's apprehension.

Influenced by Stalin and Mao's writings, Marxists began to see national liberation movements as a stage for the politics of class struggle. In brief, Marxists identified with pan-Arabism as a leading anti-Western imperialist force in the Middle East. Marxists in Egypt, for instance, sought to reposition themselves within the Egyptian pan-Arab national movement.

Notwithstanding the diversity of views among Marxists, and despite their fragmentations, they all shared certain positions. On the whole, Marxists regarded imperialism as the principal enemy. Some did not even regard Israel as a big problem because it was not seen as a sovereign independent state but rather as an imperialist dependency. A great deal of effort was exerted to project Israel as an imperialist pawn, and therefore Israel was seen as a stepdaughter (*rabiba*) of imperialism.

Despite their world view regarding the need to struggle against international imperialism, there was a dissonance among Arab Marxists on how to deal with Israel. Ever since the 1940s, two major trends of opinion dominated Marxist thinking in the Arab world, particularly in Egypt. The first trend was an ideological one that focused on theoretical issues and adopted more rigid radical positions. It viewed Israel as nothing more than a mere tool of imperialism in the region with little independence. This trend saw Israel as an aggressive Zionist entity, organically linked to international imperialism and as part of a wider political force united in its intention to control the resources of Arab countries.

The second trend adopted a pragmatic approach focusing on political reality. It viewed Israel as a society with potential for social contradictions and political manifestations. Seen from this perspective, this trend viewed Israel as a class society and emphasized the importance of alliance with some progressive social forces within Israel.

Yet, there was an agreement among all Marxist factions that Israel, since its inception, was a function of colonialism and international imperialism. This line of thinking argued that Britain realized the establishment of a Jewish state in the Middle East would only promote its imperial interests in the region, including of course the important water passages to India. The responsibility for leading the imperialist camp, according to Marxist thinking, had shifted after the Second World War to the United States. This happened at a time when the importance of the region had been increasing due to the existence of oil and the rise of the Soviet Union. The Marxist Left believed that the struggle in the Middle East was against international imperialism and Zionism.

Of equal importance, the Marxist Left agreed that there was a link between the existence of Israel in the Arab region and the Arabs' inability to bring about development in the Arab world. The first ideological trend argued that development was not possible as long as Israel undermined the efforts for development by allying itself with international imperialism. The Marxists assumed that Israel realized that a sustainable development of Arab societies would shorten the distance to the liberation of Palestine. The second trend, however, made the case for the primacy of development and for getting rid of internal exploitation over the conflict. There was no point in the Arabs fighting with Israel while they still had to suffer the presence of their impotent ruling regimes. They argued that a parasitic petty bourgeoisie in Egypt, for instance, was exploiting the masses and leading to the increase of American influence in the region. The American imperialist role could be reduced, according to this trend, by adopting good governance within the Arab world. Only then could the Arab world better manage the conflict with Israel.

These differences of opinion among Marxists led to two different perspectives. The first perspective argued that the Zionist entity should come to an end. This segment of Marxists did not advocate liquidating the Jews, but were opposed to what they regarded as the racist nature of the Zionist settler state. They were in favor of establishing a secular, democratic Palestinian state in which both Jews and Arab could peacefully coexist. This trend did not believe in the possibility of coexistence with the Zionist entity due to its expansionist nature and links to imperialism. Some advocates of this trend accepted the idea of a Palestinian state in the West Bank and Gaza as a gradual stage, but the ultimate goal remained a secular, democratic Palestinian state in all of historic Palestine. In contrast, the second trend of Marxism, did not rule out the possibility of coexisting with Israel, and accepting a two-state solution. The hope was that if this plan was implemented, the expansionist nature of the state would fade away in the future.

The Marxist Left has different readings nowadays. But the hegemony of the Marxist and pan-Arabist discourse was very salient in writing on Israel. What interests me here, and this is the crux of the matter, is that Marxists and pan-Arabists shared a few significant concepts that help to explain why writing on Israel took the shape it did. Both pan-Arabism and Arab Marxists produced the hegemonic discourse on Israel that proved to be enduring even after the demise of both ideologies with the shattering defeat of 1967.

Key Concepts

At the heart of pan-Arabist, and indeed Leftist discourse, are key recurrent concepts and assumptions that, taken together, conditioned much of the interpretation of Israel. These are anti-colonialist, anti-imperialist and insistent on the organic link between Israel (Zionism) and the imperialist world. Despite the differences between colonialism and imperialism, Arab authors used the terms interchangeably. To them they represented the highest vices that should be confronted and contained. In fact, struggle against these phenomena was not confined to the Arab world but was a trend witnessed worldwide. Thus, the context was the Third World national liberation movements (NLMs). The most paramount objective for all national liberation movements was to roll back colonialism, to achieve independence and to regain dignity. In *A Dying Colonialism*, Frantz Fanon makes the case that the essence of revolutions is a struggle for dignity and not for bread.[7] Leaders taught the masses to reject colonialism. Writing in another book, *The Wretched of The Earth* (the best known fiery indictment of colonialism), Fanon tells us that modern medical techniques brought in by imperial forces were rejected by Algerians. The "cultured imperialists" were baffled by this rejection by what they saw as ignorant, backward and stubborn Algerians. Indeed, they failed to understand the importance of dignity to the colonized people. This was very true especially in countries like Egypt. Nasser and his comrades made it a priority to get rid of the British from Egypt and were not much concerned with Israel at the beginning. The ultimate objective for the revolution and for the masses was to achieve independence. For that purpose, people were ready to concede a great deal.

Yet, whilst the national liberation movement's position was a clear-cut indictment and a blank condemnation of colonialism, the Marxist position on colonialism was very complex. It is worth briefly exploring Marx's position vis-à-vis colonialism. Karl Marx saw greater benefit from colonization in the long run that overshadowed the moral and humanitarian arguments against colonization. Colonization was seen as a historical force that would facilitate the transition to socialism. Similar to Hegel's claim that Africa had no history, Marx made the same argument with regard to Asia. In his words: "Asia had no history or at least a not known history. What we call its history, is about the history of successive intruders who founded their empires on the passive basis of that unresisting and unchanging society."[8] In fact, Marx saw colonial Britain as fulfilling a historical role in taking India from an unchanging society and dragging it into real history. He believed that Asiatic society would be changed by direct intervention from Western colonialism because capitalism would destroy the Asiatic mode of production simply by creating private properties of land. In his writings, Marx made it clear that colonialism was a dialectical process. On the one hand, it was a pitiless system of economic exploitation, but on the other hand, it was a necessary measure to destroy the pre-capital modes of production.[9]

That said, Marx held a different view of the destructive nature of colonialism in Ireland. Ireland was stunned by the British invasion and was consequently pushed back centuries.[10] In his seminal book, *Capital*, Marx provides a thorough analysis of how capitalists and landlords in Ireland collaborated to exploit the indigenous Irish and retard the process of development.[11] However, Marx remained convinced that the capitalist mode of production destroyed the pre-capitalist mode of production and unwittingly paved the way for progress, thus working as a catalyst for development.

Marx himself never wrote on imperialism because this international phenomenon only crystallized after his death. Although Marxists are very critical of imperialism, there were two main underlying meanings of imperialism which they found to be particularly unpleasant. The first meaning is associated with Lenin's *Imperialism: the Highest Stage of Capitalism*. In this important pamphlet on imperialism, Lenin sees it as a specific stage of capitalism in which centers of capital vie with colonies for expansion. The world is completely divided up among the centers of capital and land can only be passed from one owner to another.[12] The second Marxist theory on imperialism is the one associated with Karl Kautsky who sees imperialism in terms of a relationship of exploitation and domination within a world system divided between developed and underdeveloped economies.[13] The latter economy is seen as being either static or else forced to decline as a result of the relationship of dominance and exploitation. Post-colonial critics use the term imperialism in this sense rather than Lenin's and describe it as an unequal dialectic between the periphery and the core. Arab Marxists, as a consequence, despised imperialism and anything that was associated with it.

Classical Marxists did not view nationalism favorably. Bryan Turner cites Engel's (a co-writer with Marx himself) belittling of the Algerian revolt (1832–1846) against French colonization as a desperate struggle of "the barbarian state of society".[14] The reason for this loathing should be set against the background of the Marxist understanding of the importance of progress and the belief that colonization could bring about a desired outcome (destroying the pre-capitalist mode of production). Nonetheless, from a post-colonial perspective, both nationalism and Marxism had one thing in common: they both loathed colonialism and imperialism. After the institutionalizing of the Cold War (the establishment of NATO and the Warsaw Pact) and the decline of old European imperial powers in the Middle East, Marxists began to take the importance of *realpolitik* into account. In their struggle against the capitalist West, they began to see national liberation movements (NLMs) as a positive power for containing the spread of imperialism and capitalism. From a neo-Marxist perspective, NLMs radically challenged two important elements of modern imperialism: the pro-Western and pro-capitalist homegrown bourgeoisie and the international corporation. This conceptual shift beefed up Nasser's standing in the Soviet scheme. It was then, with the rapprochement between Nasser and the Soviet Union, that Arab Marxists began to position themselves within the broad pan-Arab nationalism, one that viewed Israel as an extension of imperialism which should thus be fought tooth and nail and be checked.

Evidently, both Arab Marxist and pan-Arabists have largely seen eye to eye on the link between imperialism and Zionism. Seen in this way, the notion of Israel as an imperialist–colonialist country and a tool of Western imperialism is an often-reiterated one in much of the writing on Israel in the 1950s and 1960s. Numerous books were written underpinning the key role of colonialism in establishing Israel and the major role played by imperialism in underwriting Israel with all it needed to remain powerful. From there, the 'functional' concept entered some Arab writing on Israel. This concept refers to the role of Israel in the region as servant to the interests of the imperial West. Abdelwahab Elmessiri, one of the best known Arab experts on Israel, though an Islamist, adopts this functional paradigm in explaining and dealing with the question of Zionism and Israel. Volumes are needed to fully discuss Elmessiri's ideas. Let it suffice it here to examine the main argument that informs his general analysis and understanding. In his encyclopedia on Zionism, Elmessiri presents a new way of looking at the creation of Israel. He employs the 'functional group' paradigm and argues that Israel could be seen as a functional state.[15] He argues that Jews, as a minority, served a functional role in European societies occupying positions and crafts that other members of European societies were not keen to do. They made huge amounts of money and were in turn taxed by the state. Jews were looked at with contempt and resentment by the other members of their societies. The historical break point of this group came when modern nation states with all their modern institutions came into being. These new institutions took over many of the tasks and functions that had been assigned to these functional groups. In other words, Jews' skills were no longer useful, thus devaluing their worth in society. The establishment of Israel, according to Elmessiri, was as a functional state. In other words its raison d'être was to serve the interests of imperial powers. The logical conclusion of this reasoning is that Western countries will support the survival and security of Israel as a quid pro quo for Israel fulfilling its function, namely serving Western and imperial interest in the region.

The role of Israel and imperialism was seen, by Leftists and pan-Arabists alike, as to perpetuate the state of 'backwardness' of Arab societies. Therefore, the role of Israel was to carry out policies to realize the imperial interests; dividing and emasculating the Arab world. The most repeated claims therefore, are tied to the perspective that Israel's existence had a fundamental role in protecting the interests of the imperialists, including oil, the annexation of Palestinian lands and the securing of British control over the Suez Canal in order that Britain gain access to India and the rest of the world. In addition, another imperialist interest was identified as being to establish an alien entity to guarantee the separation between the western and eastern parts of the Arab world. This was to obstruct the Arabs' progress by sidetracking them into confronting the Zionist threat, and would emasculate the Arab national liberation movement. Indeed, the Left and pan-Arabists argued that the war of 1967 was meant to fulfill Israel's functional role in the region by striking hard at pan-Arabism. Therefore, Israel's foreign policy and the functional role of this artificial state is what is important. The outcome of this assumption is the relegation of the issue of the study of Israel from within. The central problem with these assumptions is that they prevent the establishment of sound Arab scholarship on Israel. There are some elements of truth in talking about the symbiotic relationship and the mutual benefits shared by Israel and imperial powers, but dismissing the fact that Israel is independent of that is a pitfall that has contributed to the hegemony of a certain mindset which has created a distorted prism. The problem with this analysis is that it glosses over the internal workings of Israel. Even those few studies which looked at Israel from within, came up with predetermined conclusions that reduced Israel to its functional role serving Western imperialism, as though Israel will cease to exist once the Western powers' interest shifted somewhere else.

The Text

As clarified earlier in this book, text is a reflection of discourse. In other words, what is written on Israel is highly informed by the dominant ideological discourse. Seen from this perspective, much of what is written on Israel is a reflection of a certain mindset and a belief system that is conditioned by the discourse. Here the discourses are the pan-Arabist and the Leftist. It should be pointed out that there is difficulty in labeling writers (Islamists, pan-Arabists or even liberal), mainly because writers usually adopt a variety of concepts from a wide range of discourses. So whenever I use a writer as a sample, it does not mean that the writer is exclusively a member of a certain trend, but in Gramscian parlance, the hegemony of the discourse is so compelling that writers find it hard to set themselves free from its intellectual constraints.

The Pan-Arabism trend, which includes pan-Arab groups such as Nasserism, the Socialist Arab Ba'ath Parties, the Arab national movements and the Marxist groups, has contributed in delineating the boundaries of how to study Israel and what kind of conclusions should be drawn. Many of the studies were indeed on the Arab–Israeli conflict and the position towards Zionism rather than on Israel. What is common among them is that Israel is perceived as an advanced outpost for imperialism. Simply put, the writers view Israel as a force borne out of imperialism. Studies appearing in the Arab world portray Israel and imperialism as two faces of the same coin. This perspective was reinforced by Israel's actions and alliance with Western great powers that reached its peak when Israel conspired with two hated imperial powers, Britain and France, in 1956 against Nasser. From an Arab perspective, this was a clear manifestation of Israel's role in the region: to serve the objectives of the great powers against the Arab national liberation movement. Israel was seen as representing the forces of old and new colonization.

These types of plots do not surprise Arab writers. Indeed, they often link this plot to the Balfour Declaration and even the era before. It is worth pointing out an important episode that Arab writers invoke to vindicate their claim of an organic link between Zionism and colonization. They often refer to the Campbell-Bannerman Report of 1907. This report written by a committee of social scientists from different countries – Britain, France, Belgium, Holland, Portugal, Italy and Spain – was put forward to examine ways to ward off the demise of colonization. It recommended splitting the African part of the Arab world from the Asian part of the Arab world by establishing a human barrier that bridged Asia and Africa.

The report, submitted to British Liberal Prime Minster Sir Henry Campbell-Bannerman in 1907, stated that areas that were inhabited by Arabs and Muslims under the Ottoman Empire posed a genuine threat to Europe and colonization. For this reason, the document recommended the following points: firstly, the division and fragmentation of the region; secondly, the creation of artificial entities under the supervision and control of the imperialist powers; thirdly, fighting against Arab unity; and finally, and most importantly, the need to create a strong buffer state in Palestine populated by foreign people who would be antagonistic to their neighbors and a friend to imperial powers and their interests.[16] Seen from this perspective, Israel and Zionism was a function of the European need for colonization and not a matter of Jewish history itself.[17] This is one indication of how this form of interpretation of Israel and Zionism that viewed Israel as dependent of the West became ideological instead of scientific, assuming as it does a constant alliance between Zionism and Britain, and ignoring the changing nature of British interests in the region.

I shall now turn to a representative selection of Arab texts on Israel, which shed light on the mainstream academic scholarship. The objective here is to further explore particular arguments and examples of how a dominant perspective defines author positions and thus both the interpretation and the language of the scholarly inquiry on Israel.

In their book, *Israel: An Aggressive Base*, Mohammed Ali Mohammed and Ibrahim al-Himssani make the case that Israel was a forward outpost for imperialism. In their words: "in the opinion of the leaders of Western countries, Israel is a frontier outpost or a launching pad for the Western countries in the Middle East to realize their interests. Thus, Israel is a bridge to the Middle East… it is only for these reasons that the West helped establish Israel and lent it with supportive conditions to enable it to prevail."[18] It is important to understand the context of the book. The authors present their view with regard to the tripartite aggression against Egypt in 1956. It is kind of an Egyptian perspective on the war but also written mainly to take issue and refute declarations made by Moshe Dayan.[19] Again the authors see their roles as being to score points against the enemy and to scandalize rather than to explain Israel. To prove their point, these writers do not quote opposing views. They only refer to authors with perspectives sympathetic to the Arab case. Israelis are quoted mainly to vindicate the authors' perspective. Citing Israelis in such a way gives strength and vigor to these authors. A similar theme is echoed in Habib Qahwaji's book *Israel: America's Dagger*. The author argues that Israel is nothing more than a servant of American interest in the region. In his words: "the expression that is sometimes used in our Arab press and its political literature in describing Israel as a watch dog and a tool for imperialism is not without content and not out of theorizing. It is the truth."[20]

Israel's future, according to this discourse is doomed. It is just an episode in the long history of the on/off foreign domination of the area that started with the Crusaders, the Ottomans and colonization and is now represented by Israel. That said, this perspective is only adopted by the extremist end of the same discourse. Some have changed their positions according to the changing reality in the region over time. The extremist pan-Arabist trend sees the Zionist/pan-Arabist interaction as a zero-sum game in which Zionism will disappear. Obviously, this trend has failed to change the nature of the confrontation and was defeated. It is now confined to being a kind of ideological shouting. This trend has evolved to the point where it believes that Israel will not disappear and that peaceful coexistence between Arabs and Jews is possible within a secular Palestinian state without Zionism and without links to an imperialist core.

A book from a series called "We Chose For You" entitled *Zionism in the International Arena*, written by Mohammed Abd-almu'iz Nasr, echoes these points. In the background of the book's cover is a picture of a snake in the form of an Israeli flag, hissing poisonously, thus clearly indicating that it is a written indictment of Zionism. The animosity towards Zionism is justified given the conflict and the way Israel uprooted almost one million refugees from their homes (an Arab claim that is rejected by Israeli academics and politicians alike, with the exception of the New Historians who, after working in Israeli archives, lent credibility to many of the Arab claims).[21]

The book's basic ideas demonstrate the author's bias and promotion of a particular ideology. Chapter Three, for instance, is dedicated to Zionism and colonization. While it is true that there was a strong link between Britain's interest in the Middle East and the Zionist movement, it is an over-exaggeration to assume that Zionism's role was solely to serve the British interest in the region. While Britain played an indispensable role in facilitating the establishment of a homeland for the Jews in Palestine in compliance with the Balfour Declaration and with the wider strategic interest of Britain, Britain and the Zionist movement were soon at odds. Indeed, the Zionists fought Britain in the post-Second World War period to achieve a state of their own. However, this suggestion has led to the assumption, cherished by many Arab scholars, that if imperial powers were to adopt a hands-off policy, Israel would come to an end, an interpretation that assumes the internal strength of Israel's society can be ignored. To drive this point home, it is worth quoting Mohammed Abd-almu'iz Nasr at length.

> The British declared that 14 May 1948 would be the last day of their mandate in Palestine while the Jews announced that specific date would be their first one under the banner of their new state – Israel. The whole world was amazed by this news and this event. The world lived for a period of time between believing and disbelieving and people in the west and the east wondered, is that possible? Can the Jews establish a state among states? Have the Arabs weakened to the extent that they let the Jews impose their authority over an Arab district?[22]

This paragraph also indicates the general ignorance of the internal workings of the Jewish community in Palestine, known as the *Yishuv*. There was no attempt on the part of Arab scholars to understand the *Yishuv* and its institutions. For this reason, they miscalculated and had to fight a war with no knowledge of the other. Nasr's book completely ignores the domestic political inputs in Israel's (the Zionists') foreign policy, and ultimately accepts the concept of conspiracy and that everything was already planned. He also dedicates a section to the *Protocols of the Elders of Zion* as proof of the Jews' plot to dominate the world.

Another book from the same series is driven by the assumption that the organic and symbiotic relationship between Zionism and colonization is one and the same. The book is written by Dr Taha Ahmed Sharaf and entitled

Israel is a Product of Colonization. The book focuses on refuting the Jewish claims for a national homeland and the principles of the Balfour Declaration. Unsurprisingly, there is no attempt in this book to unpack Zionism as a movement. Indeed, these writers have been guided by the prevalent political and ideological atmosphere. Israel's foreign policy is a function of its place as a bastion of imperialism; therefore there is no need to analyze the internal workings of Zionism. Again, writings on Zionism were not meant to provide an objective understanding of the topic under study but rather to expose this movement as nothing but a product of colonial powers' interest in the region. To understand the fighting mood of the book, it is worth quoting this specific paragraph:

> The catastrophe of Palestine in 1948 had ended in the establishment of what they futilely called "Israel", the expulsion of one million Arab indigenous inhabitants, and the distribution of the rest of Palestine between Jordan and Egypt. Jordan annexed what fell into its hands of Palestine, while Egypt managed the Gaza Strip to give it back after the liquidation of Israel, an objective that would hopefully be realized soon.[23]

Implicit in this quote is the writer's stand vis-à-vis other Arab countries such as Jordan that were seen by pan-Arabists and Leftists as collaborators with Zionism and imperialism (more on this point in Chapter Four). It is interesting to understand the political regional context in which the writer operated. It was the second half of the 1950s, at the onset of what Malcolm Kerr called the Arab Cold War.[24] The writer preserves the same tone of exposing Britain and its role in helping the Zionists establish a homeland for themselves in order to serve Britain's interest. He considers the establishment of Israel as an international scandal and a British crime. Based on his analysis, Sharaf comes to the conclusion that regaining Palestine will only take place after a bitter conflict, not only with the Zionists, but also with Western colonization.[25]

The problem with this kind of writing is that it fails to see Israel and Zionism in any other framework. As a corollary, the book offers no understanding of the strengths and the weaknesses of Zionism and Israel. It fails also to offer an Arab scheme for how to reverse history. The authors repeatedly call for the need to rectify the historic injustice but never say how or whether this is possible given the prevalent balance of power and the Arab strategic vulnerability. This book is yet another example of the dominance of certain discourses that limit both epistemology and the ontology of the topic under study. The prism of the conflict was so salient that it did not help the writer to go beyond the immediate need to scandalize the Zionist–colonialist collaboration. Simply put, the writer subscribed to the assumption that the most important aspect of Israel is its foreign policy, which could be wholly understood by studying the imperial interest in the region. There was no attempt on his part to unpack the society and to try to present a thorough explanation of Israel's behavior in the region. Israel, according to this mode of thinking, was seen as a unitary political entity. In other words, there were no meaningful differences among the different political constituents of this entity; all of them wanted to expand. In Nasser's own analysis, the only difference among them was that the Israeli opposition sought expansion to incorporate the 'promised land' from the Nile to the Euphrates whereas the Labor government sought to impose peace by force.[26] In *This is Zionism*, a book written by Israel Cohen (described by Nasser as a zealot Zionist) and translated and published in Cairo in 1954, Nasser himself wrote a foreword yet there was no indication that the book was translated from another language. It is an interesting approach quoting Nasser in the introduction of the book. In Nasser's words:

> This book was originated by one of the Zionist zealots (Israel Cohen) in which he tells the story of Zionism from a Zionist perspective. He believes in what he says or pretends to do so in order to deceive international public opinion. He may be correct in some of what he says or may be lying in all of it. It does not matter as we are only interested in knowing the story of Zionism as told by one of them so that our knowledge of it will improve our awareness and help us in future struggles.[27]

After telling the story of Zionism, the editor of the book includes an epilogue that presents this book to the Arab reader and seeks to enlighten them about their number one enemy – the colonial powers. He ranks these enemies as follows: the British and their American allies, followed by the Jews, and concludes with other enemies within Eastern and Western Europe. He builds the case for the fact that the main interest of these powers was to render the Arabs powerless and get rid of the "Jewish morbid growth in their bodies". This was why they supported the Jews in establishing a state for themselves in Palestine.[28]

Central to writing in the 1950s and 1960s is the hegemonic perspective that links Israel and Zionism to colonialism. Unsurprisingly, a key component of pan-Arabist and Leftist perspective was a hostility to Western influence in the region. Israel is seen as a stepdaughter (*rabiba*) of imperial powers. In *Israel: An Aggressive Base*, the authors highlight the functional role of Israel as serving imperial interests. In its introduction, the book labels Israel as a *rabiba* for American colonization. There are many flaws in this argument. To begin with, there was no American colonization in the Middle East when this book was written. The authors' use of terminologies are, to say the least, incorrect. According to the book, Israel is nothing more than an outpost for the imperial countries to achieve their objectives in the region.[29] Again, the writing here is not used as a means for understanding but rather as a means of scoring points and scandalizing the other.

This mode of writing (Israelism) has long ignored the internal working of Israel as irrelevant. The outcome was gross ignorance of Israeli society and politics. This period extended from 1948 until 1967, and could be characterized as a period of ignorance of Israel from within. The number of books on Israel was modest, but more importantly, writing was a way to mobilize confrontation with Zionism, Israel and the imperial powers in the region. The problem with this period was that studying Israel was seen as a luxury or as a way to establish intimacy with the other at a time when the objective was to delegitimize Israel. Approaching Israel from within was a kind of nationalist pollution that should not take place.[30] Israel was looked at as an entity and not as a state with classes and political forces.

Undoubtedly, some authors studied internal politics in Israel. But the purpose of the study was to vindicate the link with major powers or to say how to inflict a defeat on Israel. Almost a decade and a half elapsed before writers began to pay attention to the significance of internal dynamics in

Israel. In a book published in Egypt, Ali Mohammed Ali criticizes what he deems as a lack of knowledge on Israel. He argues that even fifteen years after the establishment of Israel, there was not a single book that offered the Arab readership a complete study on Israel and its political and economic entities.[31] He rightly argues that the Arabs lost the war against Israel because they knew little about it. He takes it upon himself to rectify the mistake the Arabs paid dearly for in 1948.

Whilst there is an element of truth in his claim, his book offers nothing but propaganda and weak scholarship. Part of the book can be seen as a fact sheet providing background information on Israel and its political system in a factual manner. However, the author did not follow good scholarship when he offered his interpretations. At one point, he talks about the issue of Israel as a "cancer" in the Arab world. This simile has been used among Arab writers arguing that nothing short of the eradication of the cancer would enable the body, i.e. the Arab world, to function properly. Ali Mohammed Ali however maintains that a cancer comes from within the body and there is no satisfactory cure to this disease. In many cases cancer will put an end to the body. Put differently, he indicates that referring to Israel as a cancer is like giving in to its existence. Mohammed Ali, on the other hand, argues that Israel is instead an alien entity that will soon be rejected and come to an end. His argument is that Israel is not an intractable cancer and the decisive remedy is already well known – the liquidation of Israel.[32] After offering his journalistic reading of the Israeli economy, he comes to the conclusion that Israel would not have survived were it not for foreign aid. To him, it is a state that relied on foreign aid and loans and therefore does not have the preconditions to last. Needless to say, his study of the economy is impressionistic and lacks scientific analysis. Although foreign aid was important to Israel, as it was to many other countries, Israel would have survived without massive aid. The problem is that a large number of scholars have been driven by a kind of wishful thinking or are influenced by the inevitability syndrome. As a further indication of this, Ali Mohammed Ali also argues that the Arabs are on their way to achieving unity and that once this has been achieved then there will be hope of putting an end to Israel.[33]

It is true that Israel would not have come into being were it not for British help, starting with the Balfour Declaration in the interwar period and beyond. The *Yishuv*, for instance, was a subject of internal debate that led to a split in the Zionist Organization and the emergence of a revisionist strand of Zionism. Certainly, the Jewish leaders of the *Yishuv* exploited the imperial interests in the region but their objective was always an independent Jewish state. The same is applicable during the Cold War era. Israel used the Cold War and the global rivalry between the Soviet Union and the United States to further its own national interests. So did the Arabs. Israel's decision to align itself to the United States was seen as a kind of security guarantee rather than any indication of automatic service to the patron.[34]

Implicit, and sometimes explicit, in Arab scholars' writing is the conviction that Israel's resilience in the region is a function of imperial interests rather than because of Israel itself. The over-reliance of the perceived link between imperialism and Israel proved to be an intellectual trap for many well-known scholars. Nasr Shamali and Hisham

Al-Dajani put forward a thesis in a book that belittles the trend of focusing on internal politics stating that internal politics is nothing more than a response to the external environment. This is not entirely incorrect. They went as far as warning about the trend in analysis for studying Israeli politics independent of American politics. They add that the Israeli political parties, particularly the large ones, are a major part of the multifaceted arrangements that exist to serve the global capitalist system. They published a book addressing the Likud electoral victory in 1977. The tasks of Israeli parties, according to them, are confined to creating a socio-political atmosphere that positions Israelis in a suitable place for carrying out their duties in serving the international system in the best way. They were gathered in Palestine to realize this particular objective. In their words: "many have believed that the ascendance of Likud to power was a complete and comprehensive turnabout in Israeli politics. They based their belief on their knowledge of history and the platform of the extremist right-wing Herut Party. However, they soon discovered that the difference between one party and another in Israel is confined, by and large, to formal matters. Likud has accomplished political tasks that were supposed to be of Labor's affairs."[35]

They conclude that the task of the Israeli parties in Israel is to control the society, with all its diversities and discrepancies, and get it ready to serve the interests of the international capitalist system. To them, that was the norm. They warn that if there were some deviation from this norm, the parties would be trivial and ineffective. Evidently, the authors fail to see the policies inherent in the directions of the settlement activities after the ascendance of Likud to power, and the prominence of the settler *Gush Emunim* (the Block of Faithful) movement and how that led to the plantation of hundreds of thousands of settlers and scores of settlements in a direct clash with their patron's (the United States) foreign policy regarding settlement and how this obstructed the peace process. To them, even peace with Egypt, which was of paramount security importance to Israel as it took the southern front (the most dangerous from Israel's strategists' point of view) out of the conflict, was a proof of the controllability of the society in serving the strategy of the global capitalist stem.

Such texts have miserably failed to take into account the important role of ideology and the psychological components of the Israeli decision makers. It is almost impossible to understand Begin's foreign policy, for example, without exploring his mindset. Begin's belief system was highly informed by the teachings of Jabotinsky and the dominance of the Holocaust on his political consciousness. Therefore, the notion that Israeli foreign policy only served the imperial interests is, to say the least, reductionist and incorrect in most cases. To their credit, the authors document internal changes accurately and in a systematic way. However, it is not a matter of insufficient information about what was taking place in 1977, as much as it is a matter of interpretation.

I do not want to bring all writers and authors together under this somewhat rigid categorization. Some writers that belong to the Left and pan-Arab discourse defy this profiling. Some excellent Arab scholars (like Habib Qahawaji) have managed epistemologically to go beyond the conflict and break with the ideological impediments of the pan-Arabist and Leftist discourse and study Israel objectively from within. Paradoxically, Azmi Bishara (an Arab Israeli professor and

Knesset member who is seen in Israel as anti-Israel and more pan-Arabist) has written soundly on Israel.[36] While maintaining his position that Israel is an aggressive country that continues to be governed by some racist behaviors and discriminate against part of its citizenship, Bishara offers a sound analysis of Israeli politics giving primacy to the significance of internal variables and politics. It is likely that Israeli intellectuals will take issue with some of Bishara's analytical concepts, but the fact remains that the book is a result of the author's deep involvement and understanding of the internal scene in Israel. In some parts of the book, Bishara mocks a segment of Arab scholars who make the case that internal politics of Israel is nothing more than a play in which the main actors divide roles.[37] Bishara insists that a cultural, economic, social and class struggle is ongoing in Israel and revolves around power and authority. It is this strife that determines much of Israel's foreign policy in the region rather than the simplistic idea that Israel serves the interests of imperial powers. Simply put, nothing short of unpacking Israel from within can help to offer a sound analysis of Israeli behaviors in the region.

Despite Bishara's vigorous analysis in his book, the publisher of the book is the Center for Arab Unity Studies based in Beirut. The foreword written by the center is rather ideological and fails to read the book correctly, it reads: "The book is a document that condemned the Hebrew state."[38] Clearly, the publisher could have chosen neutral words, yet their ideological stand and their deep-seated desire to bring what they see as the Israeli racist nature to the fore is overt. Of course, the publishers are not close to the author in terms of understanding the topic under discussion, nor do they match his well-known intellectual talents. Yet the center, which is known for promoting the idea of Arab unity, allows its ideological stand to color the very first few pages thus impacting greatly on the understanding of its Arab readers.

Conclusion

This chapter has illustrated that the hegemony of the discourse created an intellectual and ideological framework that proved detrimental to a sound analysis of the topic under study. Arab scholarly interpretation of Israel was hardly impartial and often linked to certain epistemological perspectives. The latter constitutes the prism through which Israel was studied and analyzed. The pan-Arabist and Leftist hegemonic discourses were ideological in nature thus creating boundaries of how and what should be studied. The overwhelming bulk of Israelism, particularly in the period between the establishment of Israel and the war in 1967, was in compliance with the hegemonic pan-Arabist and Leftist discourses. Central to this period are concepts such as imperialism and the organic link with Zionism and Israel as a *rabiba* or *laqitta* (illegitimate daughter). The concept of Israel as a state, which determines its moves from within, was missing from the analysis.

As mentioned earlier in Chapter One, Arab scholars at the time were under severe pressure due to the ongoing conflict with Israel, and to the declared objective that was to put an end to this illegitimate entity in Palestine. Over the first two decades of the conflict, relations with Israel were indeed seen as a zero-sum game. Few, if any, studies looked at Israel from within. Even the few that did, were conducted to vindicate the link between Zionism and imperialism. This ideological trap caused the Arabs damage by inhibiting understanding of Israel from within, and reducing scholarly work to a propagandist form aimed at mobilizing the masses blindly behind authoritarian regimes.

It should be emphasized here that the appeal of pan-Arabist and Leftist discourses declined after the war in 1967. Although the legacy of the first two decades prevailed for a while through certain concepts, it soon gave way, or became secondary to the rising discourse of political Islam, which will be discussed in the next chapter.

Scientific approaches known in social sciences were absent when it came to the study of Israel. Writing was reactive, tense and propagandist. Had the Arab writers put aside their political and ideological perspectives and their animosity toward Israel and instead studied Israel in a more scholarly manner, results would have been different in terms of understanding. Unfortunately, even the 'know your enemy' approach that prevailed after 1967 failed to decouple the role of the conflict and the ideological entrenchment from the topic under study. In a nutshell, Arab writing on Israel has always proceeded with certain preconditions.

That said, sound and sophisticated analysis should explore the interplay between internal political dynamics and the role of external factors such as the American and Arab positions. External factors can certainly enhance or decrease the level of internal party contradictions. But in the final analysis, there is no single variable that can account for Israel's behavior in the region. Put differently, the trend of analysis that focuses on the link between Zionism and imperialism should be dismissed for a multi-level approach that focuses on the interaction between domestic politics and foreign policy.[39]

Notes

—　—

1　Joel Beinin, *Was the Red Flag Flying There? Marxist Politics and the Arab–Israeli Conflict in Egypt and Israel, 1948–1965* (Berkeley and Los Angeles: University of California Press, 1990).

2　Sati al-Husri, *Ma Hiya al-Qawmiya: Abhath wa Disrasat 'ala Dhaw'l al-Ahdath wa al-Nadhariyat* (What is Nationalism?: Enquiries and Studies in light of events and theories) (Beirut: Dar al-'ilm li al-Malayeen, 1963).

3　*Ibid.*

4　Joel Beinin, *Was the Red Flag Flying There?*, p. 24.

5　*Hashomer hatza'ir* was a political party in the pre-state era that advocated a bi-national solution in Palestine with equality between the Jews and the Arabs. This party voted against the Biltmore Program in 1942, which called for the establishment of a state for the Jews. Later it merged with MAPAM, which in turn became part of today's Meretz.

6　Joel Beinin, *Was the Red Flag Flying There?*, p. 25.

7　Frantz Fanon, *A Dying Colonialism* (New York: Grove Press, 1965), translated from French.

8　Karl Marx, "The Future Results of British Rule in India", in *The Portable Karl Marx* (New York: Viking Press, 1983).

9　Karl Marx, *The Communist Manifesto* (New York: Washington Square Press, 1964).

10　Karl Marx and Frederick Engels, "On Ireland", in *Ireland and the Irish Question; A Collection of Writings* (New York: International Publishers, 1972).

11　Karl Marx, *Capital* (Chicago, Ill: Encyclopedia Britannica, c1952).

12　V. I., Lenin, *Imperialism, The Highest Stage of Capitalism: A Popular Outline* (Peking: Foreign Languages Press, 1965), first published 1917.

13　Karl Kautsky, *Socialism and Colonial Policy: An Analysis* (Belfast: Athol Books, 1975).

14 Bryan Turner, *Marx and the End of Orientalism* (London: George Allen & Unwin, 1978), p. 5.

15 Abdelwahab Elmessiri, *Mauso'at al-Yahud, al-Yahudiya wal Suhyuniya: Namozaj Tafsiri* (Encyclopedia of the Jews, Judaism, and Zionism: A New Explanatory Paradigm. Eight Volumes) (Cairo: Dar-Elshuruq: 1999).

16 Sami Adwan and Dan Bar-On, "Learning Each Other's Historical Narratives In Israeli and Palestinian Schools", http://www.vispo.com/PRIME/leohn.htm (Accessed 20 June 2007).

17 Zionism came into being as a function of the failure of assimilations and the rise of anti-Semitism in 19th-century Europe. It is a movement that deems Jews, who were scattered all over the world, as one nation with a historic homeland (Palestine) and hence a claim for self-determination. This is how Zionists see themselves and this is the foremost ideological underpinning of Zionism.

18 Ali Mohammed Ali and Ibrahim al-Himssani, *Israel Qa'eda 'Dwaniya* (Israel: An Aggressive Base) (Cairo: Addar Al-Qawmiyya Litiba'ah Wanahir), p. 15.

19 Moshe Dayan was the Chief of Staff during the 1956 war, who is seen as the main architect of this war. He became a Defense Minister in 1967 to help the then Prime Minister to launch a war against the Arabs.

20 Habib Qahwaji, *Israel: Khanjar America* (America's Dagger) (Damascus: Mu'sast Al-'Ard, 1979), p. 88.

21 Benny Morris, *The Birth of the Refugee Problem, 1947–49* (Cambridge: Cambridge University Press, 1987).

22 Mohammed Abd-almu'iz Nasr, *Al-Suhyuniya fil Majal 'Dawli* (Zionism in the International Arena) (Egypt: Dar al-Ma'arif, 1957), p. 5.

23 Taha Ahmed Sharaf, *Israel min Sun' 'l'isti'mar* (Israel is a Product of Colonization) (Cairo: Dar 'lma'arif), pp. 5–6.

24 For the inter-Arab rivalry and differences see Malcolm Kerr, *The Arab Cold War: Gamal 'Abd Al-Nasir and His Rivals, 1958–1970* (Oxford and New York: Oxford University Press, 1971).

25 Taha Ahmed Sharaf, *Israel min Sun' 'l'isti'mar*, p. 200.

26 Mohammed al-Sayid Saleem, *Al-Tahlil 'Siyasi 'Nasiri* (Nasserite Political Analysis) (Beirut: Markiz Dirasat Al-Wahda Al-'Rabyia, 1983), p. 153.

27 The Cultural Committee of the Editing Commission, *Hazihi 'Suhyunyiah* (This is Zionism) (Cairo: Dar al-Ma'arif, 1954), p. 10.

28 *Ibid.*, pp. 146–7.

29 Ali Mohammed Ali and Ibrahim al-Himssani, *Israel Qa'eda 'Dwaniya* (Israel: An Aggressive Base) (Cairo: Addar Al-Qawmiyya Litiba'ah Wanahir), p. 15.

30 Abdel Monem Said, *al-Ahram al-Iqtisadi (Economic Ahram)*, 23 January 2003.

31 Ali Mohammed Ali, *Fi Dakhil Israel: Dirasat Kiyanaha Al-Siyasi Wal 'Iqtisadi* (Inside Israel: A Study on its Political and Economic Entity) (Cairo), p. 3.

32 *Ibid.*, p. 3.

33 *Ibid.*, pp. 366–7.

34 Indeed whether Israel was a strategic asset or liability was debated among two schools of thought in the United States and only decided on after its spectacular victory in the war in 1967, see Avi Shlaim, *War and Peace in the Middle East*, revised and updated edition (London and New York: Penguin, 1995).

35 Nasr Shamali and Hisham Al-Dajani, *Al-Ahzab wal Kutal Asiyasyyah fi Israel* (Political Parties and Blocs in Israel) (Beirut: Maktab El-Khadamat Atiba'yah, 1986), p. 4–5.

36 Azmi resigned from the Knesset and chose to leave Israel to live in the diaspora in April 2007.

37 Azmi Bishara, *Al-Intifada wal Mujtama' Al-Israeli: Tahlil fi Khidam al-Ahdath* (The Intifada and the Israeli Society: Analysis Amid Events), p. 117.

38 *Ibid.*, p. 9.

39 Hassan A. Barari, *Israeli Politics and the Middle East Peace Process, 1988–2002* (London and New York: Routledge, 2004).

3

Religious Discourse

—‑—

Our Islamic nation is still suffering from the plots and cunning of the Jews.

Sayyid Qutb, *Our Battle with the Jews*

Israel will exist and will continue to exist until Islam will obliterate it, just as it obliterated others before it.

Hamas Charter

Introduction

In the last two chapters I have attempted to underscore the close association between an author's perspective and their writing on Israel. These perspectives are mostly derived from the persistence of the Arab–Israeli conflict and the series of military defeats that befell the Arab states in their

73

confrontation with Israel. Writing on Israel becomes a function of the hegemony of certain perspectives in the Arab world. Seen in this way, I argue that nothing short of deconstructing these discourses will enable us to comprehend why Israel is interpreted as it is.

While religious discourse existed before 1967, it was not as dominant as the pan-Arabist rhetoric. However, the 1967 war was a turning point of historic importance. Pan-Arabism received a lethal blow from which it never recovered after Nasser was defeated by Israel. The defeat was so stinging that the entire appeal of pan-Arabism was diminished. The resultant ideological vacuum was soon to be filled by political Islam in the Meshreq (countries including Egypt, Lebanon, Jordan, Syria, Palestine and Iraq). Recently, with the rise of political Islam as a credible alternative to current corrupt regimes in the region, the discourse has become even more entrenched. It should be pointed out that I will focus on the discourse of politicized Islamist movements and groups but will exclude two other streams. The first stream is the Sufi Islamic groups known in Arabic as *tarikas*. These groups are certainly apolitical. They do not interfere in issues of public interest such as the Arab–Israeli conflict. The second strand that I have excluded is what might be termed 'establishment Islam'. This kind of Islam is dependent on the state and therefore serves to justify the state's actions in theological terms. For instance, the Islamist clergies of the al-Azhar issued a *fatwa* (religious verdict) sanctioning Sadat's efforts when he opted for peace with Israel in 1977. They did so by using Islam to enhance the legitimacy of the president, citing a verse from the Qur'an that encourages a Muslim to make peace with an enemy that opted to do so. The reason for this movement's exclusion is the lack of their relative impact on Islamist movements as a whole, and the public's perception of them as an extension of the secular state.

The Ascendance of the Religious Discourse

Strikingly and despite the belated ascendance of the Islamic discourse after the war in 1967, Islamists' interest in the question of Palestine and Zionism pre-dated the emergence of the pan-Arabist and the Marxist movements in the Arab world. Mohammed Rashid Rida (1865–1935), a pioneering Islamic thinker, was perhaps the first to warn against Zionist plans in the region.[1] From the turn of the twentieth century until his death, Rida's writings in *al-Mannar* (an influential Islamic journal founded by him) stressed the need to understand the Zionist movement in order to confront it. Rida's writing reflects his deep-seated faith that Palestine, from the Mediterranean to the Jordan River, is an Islamic endowment. He therefore viewed the attempt to establish a homeland for the Jews, particularly in the wake of the Balfour Declaration, as one of the worst manifestations of colonization. In his writings, Rida pointed out the organic link between Western (British) colonization and Zionism. His strategic reading was that Britain was using the Jews in the region to emasculate the Arabs and distract their attention. This theme does not differ from either pan-Arabism or Marxism. Nevertheless, Rida established contacts with Zionists in an attempt to convince them that the Arabs were prepared to accept Jews as normal citizens in Palestine but would not agree to a Jewish state.[2]

The spiritual father and founder of the Muslim Brotherhood, Hassan al-Banna, is another more high-ranking

Islamic intellectual who took particular interest in the issue of Palestine. His interest in Palestine began to surface in the 1930s when he issued a *fatwa* allowing Muslims to direct part of their alms to *mujahdeen* (fighters) in Palestine who were fighting the Zionists.[3] It is worth noting that his actions in supporting the Palestinians came amid Egypt's preoccupation with independence and the emergence of the state system in the Middle East. Al-Banna regarded Islam and Palestine as interlinked issues and therefore focused on shaping a public opinion that viewed Palestine as an Islamic issue. He even equated saying that you had nothing to do with Palestine with saying you had nothing to do with Islam. He lobbied the Egyptian government vigorously to push the British to end Jewish immigration in order to ward off the possible scenario of evacuating the land of its Palestinian owners. Al-Banna preserved one line of thought throughout the struggle, which was his opposition to the apparently biased British policies. He even suggested the establishment of an Arab fund to buy land in Palestine in order to avert Jewish control of it. His demands were crystal clear: put an end to Jewish immigration, and gain the independence of the Arabs of Palestine in a state where Jews would be dealt with as a minority.[4] In 1948, the Muslim Brotherhood engaged in a violent encounter with the Egyptian government. Shortly afterwards in 1948, al-Banna was assassinated at the age of 44. His legacy however, remains intact to this day.

Of all Islamic intellectuals, perhaps Sayyid Qutb stands out as the most influential. His relevancy and tremendous impact was not confined to Egypt. Qutb rose to prominence in the 1950s after the demise of Hassan al-Banna despite being jailed by Nasser's regime. He used his time in prison to write what many would consider the bible of the radical movements, *Ma'alim fi al-Tariq* (Milestones).[5] While he belonged to the Muslim Brotherhood, his teachings and writings were much more radical than this organization. His intellectual contribution lies in two concepts: *hakimiyya* and *jaihillia*. The former refers to the concept of divine sovereignty and a total submission to God, whereas the latter refers to the pre-Islamic ignorance that characterized the life of the infidels. Undoubtedly, the two concepts predated Qutb and were first used by the Kharajites in the seventh century and the influential Pakistani scholar Mawdudi in the twentieth century, yet it was Qutb that gave them universal relevance. Qutb's main argument was that Arabs and Muslims live in a status of *jaihillia* and the only way to change this situation is to implement *hakimiyya*. Obviously, the tool to bring about *hakimiyya* is *jihad* (holy war).

Rida, al-Banna and Qutb all made a link between Palestine and the belief of the Islamic nation at a time of the nation-state's entrenchment. Although all three thinkers saw Israel as incapable of surviving on its own without the support of an external power, each one focused on a different level. Rida gave priority to understanding Zionism and warning the Ottoman state of its dangers. Al-Banna underscored the practical side of undermining the Zionist project in Palestine, whereas Qutb drew attention to the civilization aspect of the conflict.

Conspicuously, their discourse remained secondary to the prevailing pan-Arabist discourse, though it was salient. However, following the 1967 war there was a gradual growth in the popularity of Islamic movements amongst increasing numbers of people in the Arab world. The 1970s saw the Islamists' genie emerge from the bottle. To all practical intents, it was Anwar Sadat of Egypt who started grooming Islamic movements in an attempt to clip the wings of the Nasserites and the Leftists. Paradoxically, Sadat was unaware that the tide would become so overwhelming that he would ultimately pay with his life. Islamists assassinated him for signing a peace treaty with Israel but also for his refusal to cooperate in the Islamization of Egyptian society through the implementation of the *Sharia* (religious rule).

In an attempt to account for the rise of the Islamists, most observers agree that it can be explained by the failure of the nation state to deliver on issues such as development, the absence of a public space to voice resentments, the existence of authoritarian regimes throughout the Middle East, and the role of external factors be it colonization or encroaching secular values. The latter was seen as both corrupting and erroneous.[6] Indeed, these issues have been the key drivers in the process of shaping opposition movements in much of the Arab and Muslim world.

In the case of Islamist movements (including those in the Meshreq countries), one cannot simply gather all Islamic trends and varying schools of thoughts under one category, rubric or movement. There are many epistemological differences between them as to how the Islamization of the society should be achieved. The divergences center mainly around the means: to take up the peaceful non-violent route, or use force by seizing power and imposing change on society. It will suffice here to put forth a simple distinction that is as follows: one trend was committed to peaceful change and therefore adopted a bottom-up approach, whereas the other was radically militant and hence adopted a top-down approach.

Peaceful movements attempted to win the hearts and minds of the masses by increasing their influence through the education, social and welfare programs made possible by the oil money of the 1970s. These movements sought to Islamize the societies through preaching and charities, which would give them more influence than the militant movements.[7] Islam's prescription and focus on social justice was seen as an antidote to the authoritarian and corrupt regimes. Hamas's electoral victory in Palestine in January 2006 and the electoral success of the Muslim Brotherhood in Egypt should be seen in the light of the successful, gradual, charitable approach. Put simply, they are seen by many as an ideological alternative that is neither violent nor corrupt.

Up until 1967, the Islamists' struggle was directed mainly against secular nationalist authoritarian regimes. This was the case in Egypt where Nasser reacted by torturing and imprisoning the Islamists for extended periods of time. The Islamists' main concern was to secure the welfare of Egyptian society by implementing Islamic laws. Although a majority of these militant inmates refused to support Nasser's 1967 war efforts, the shock and humiliation of the war radicalized the younger generation outside of Egyptian prisons. The younger generation's exposure to the concepts and influence of the Islamic groups took shape within the high school and university setting. This younger generation began to shift the blame from Israel as an outside enemy to a closer enemy, the 'paganism' of Nasser and other Arab regimes.

Different Arab countries had different experiences; the Egyptian experience contrasted radically with that of Jordan. The Jordanian monarchy adopted an across-the-board strategy of inclusion in order to moderate Islamists.

In fact, when Jordan was threatened by pan-Arabism and communism in the 1950s and 1960s, Jordan used the Islamists to counter the ideological threat. The Islamists allied themselves with the regime against what they saw as the encroachment of secular values represented in pan-Arabism and communism. Therefore, unlike Egypt, Islamists in Jordan have not been through a radicalization process as the system was relatively open for them to practice their preaching and charitable work.

For many Islamists, the struggle against close enemies takes precedence over more distant enemies, such as Israel and the West. Abd al-Salam Faraj (a leader of the Jihad organization and one of the people executed for his involvement in the assassination of President Sadat) coined the theory 'The Absence Duty'.[8] This states that the real enemies are the incumbent regimes that should be fought against vehemently if the Muslims aspire to restore their dignity and Islamic society. These rulers are the lackeys of imperialism. Therefore, fighting them is far more important than liberating Jerusalem, although the liberation of the holy land is a binding precept upon any Muslim. The slogan "The road to Jerusalem runs through Cairo" was common in their rhetoric. Faraj's ideas on *jihad* became the operational code for all *jihadi* movements in Egypt during the 1980s and 1990s. Traditionally, *jihad* is a collective duty. However Faraj turned this traditional notion on its head when he claimed that *jihad* was a personal duty for each Muslim who was capable of fighting and that *jihad* should start against the Arab rulers (who were according to him, apostates).[9]

An often-reiterated theme in Faraj's literature is that Muslim land was occupied through the fault and defects of the Muslim rulers. Faraj's views on the need to liberate Jerusalem were not unique, Islamist movements on the whole share the same perspective. However this was to be achieved by waging *jihad* under the banner of an Islamic state and not under the reign of impious leadership. Hence the focus was on internal matters.[10] There was a deep-seated belief that the imminent danger for Muslims was the secular-minded regimes. These regimes were accused of being prisoners of Western ideas such as secularism and nationalism. Khomeini of Iran coined the term 'westoxication' when describing the condition of these elites that should be fought. Parallel to this Islamist perspective is what is often referred to as 'authenticity'. This concept entails a return to the past and a rejection of modernity, which is viewed as interlinked with the negative connotations of the West.

The 1970s witnessed what could be termed Islamic resurrection. The leaders of this trend belonged to the prison generation and many of them had suffered cruel torture in the prisons of the secular and nationalist regimes. Once they were out, they developed a fixation with torture and the evils of the morally corrupt secular regimes and their objective was to overthrow the regimes. Notably, the Israeli–Zionist theme featured prominently in the Islamist discourse through the convergence of two events at the end of the 1970s after which the Islamists were catapulted into prominence. The first event was Sadat's visit to Israel and the subsequent peace treaty, and the second was the Iranian revolution of 1979. Sadat's bombshell visit to Israel shocked the Islamists in a way that paralleled the defeat of 1967. This was not an easy task given the concerns of the post-1967 generation, but Sadat had crossed a red line and should therefore pay with his life. His strategy to realign Egypt with the West to regain Sinai and to introduce liberal economic steps, known in Egypt as the policy of *infitah*, to bring prosperity to the Egyptian economy as a quid pro quo, was opposed by the Islamists who viewed the struggle with Israel as a zero-sum game. The most potent Islamic organization, the Muslim Brotherhood, opposed the peace treaty vehemently.

According to the Muslim Brotherhood (whether based in the Mashreq or elsewhere), Israel represented one of three enemies and was a constant threat to the Arabs and the Muslims. The first enemy was the 'crusade' of the West, the next one was communism, the third Israel and Zionism. This mode of thinking is evident in all in-depth analysis of the Islamists' writings. What is unique in the movement's writings is that the communist threat was soon dropped during the 1990s and the Jewish threat took center stage. In Jordan for example, *al-Sabeel*, a weekly paper issued by the Muslim Brotherhood, has buzzed with articles repeating the same theme. It is hardly possible to find one issue that doesn't devote sizeable space to stressing that Israel, supported by the West, is the ultimate enemy of the Muslim nation.[11] Sadat was assassinated by Islamist groups during a military parade in October 1981.

The second event that brought the Islamists to prominence was the Islamic revolution in Iran, which filled a generation with hope and vigor and instilled in them the belief that the unthinkable could happen. It is true that the revolution was a Shiia (a major main sect of Islam but not the sect the majority of Muslims subscribe to) revolt, but it nevertheless ignited the notion in a generation that revolution could work. These two events in particular, followed by the Israeli invasion of Lebanon in 1982, made Israel and Zionism prominent themes in the discourse of fundamentalists as early as the 1980s. The Israeli assault on Lebanon was called the 'Tenth Crusade' against Islam. Israel was dubbed as the new Mongol, a reference to the Mongol attack on Baghdad in 1258 which led to the end of the Abbasid Caliphate.

Islamists' deep antipathy towards Jews, which goes back to the time of the Prophet, was fast coming to the fore. Israel's policies of occupation and its aggressive and unprovoked war in Lebanon sounded alarms among Islamists who began to see Israel as an imminent threat to Muslim societies. In the wake of Sadat's assassination, the Muslim Brotherhood in Egypt launched a campaign against normalizing relations with Israel. This campaign proved to be effective as it frightened hundreds of thousands of Egyptians who would otherwise have normalized relations with Israel. Omar Al-Tilimsani, the Supreme Guide of the Egyptian Muslim Brothers, argued that the implementation of the peace treaty with Israel should be blocked. In his words, this would reduce the evil. He viewed any Israeli presence in Egypt, or contact, as a form of cultural or economic imperialism that posed a threat to the endurance of Muslim Egypt.

The successful campaign served as a model for the Jordanian Muslim Brotherhood when it spearheaded a campaign against normalization with Israel during the second half of the 1990s. The anti-normalization committee in Jordan published a blacklist containing the names of people who had normalized relations with Israel. This campaign was not initially effective. However, with the impasse in the peace process and what Jordanian saw as aggressive Israeli policies, more and more Jordanians conformed to the thinking of the committee.[12]

When the militant *jihadi* movements failed to bring about a change in the enemy close at hand they switched to

83

the distant enemy and went global.[13] Ayman al-Zawahiri's *Knights under the Prophet's Banner* is the most politically grounded and comprehensive manifesto on global *jihad*. He began with a call to move *jihad's* target from the near enemy to the far away enemy.

In essence, despite the existence of a plethora of Islamic movements and the bifurcation of views among them, they all shared certain assumptions vis-à-vis Israel. These assumptions constituted the structural and historical thinking of the Islamists' vision regarding Jews and by extension Israel and Zionism.

Basic Concepts and Writings

It is worth pointing out that not all authors that fall under this category are necessarily Islamists. Some of them are certainly not. Yet their writing is peppered with references to old images of Jews during Mohammed's time. These images remain set in stone in the thoughts and writings of Islamists, and have not been subject to reconsideration.

More than anything else, Islamists see the conflict between the Arabs and Israel in the context of the historic conflict between Jews and Muslims. It is not a conflict over borders, as moderates would prefer to put it, but a conflict concerning existence. This zero-sum approach leads them to argue that peace and coexistence with Israel is simply impossible. To some of them, there is no 'middle of the road' strategy or solution. They project the conflict as though it were an extension of the Jews' hostile position vis-à-vis all prophets and particularly Mohammed. Saad Eddin Ibrahim, a prominent Egyptian sociologist, has contributed to our understanding of the domestic developments in Egypt and has analyzed the Islamists' political position vis-à-vis Israel. He writes: "this group views Israel as a theocratic state which is racist, exclusivist, expansionist and evil... Israel should be fought until the land of historic Palestine is completely liberated... the models of their approach are Hamas and Hezbollah."[14] Elsewhere, Saad Eddin wrote: "The Muslim Brotherhood's arguments revolve around the impossibility of peaceful coexistence with the Jewish state. It is an aggressor on *dar al-islam* [the region of Islam]. Israel, directly or indirectly, has been the cause of the major calamities befalling Muslims everywhere, especially in Palestine. It has desecrated Muslim shrines in the Holy Land. And as an evil, it must be eradicated."[15]

They all agree that Israel is to disappear someday and therefore they are exponents of Israel's eventual obliteration. That said, they differ among themselves over how to bring about the Islamization of Arab societies. Their discourse has proved to be enduring, especially during the last decade. The hegemony of their discourse was so strong that it has created a kind of McCarthyism in writing on Israel, making any thinking outside of the box nigh impossible. They often juxtapose the past and the present in a rigid manner as though the present is a mirror image of the past, for example when comparing Israel to the crusader states of centuries ago. In addition, they view Israel and Zionism as a force that has driven Western imperialism and international communism into the Middle East.

It is hardly surprising that the level of mutual enmity between Muslims and Jews dates back centuries. From the Muslim standpoint, since the Jews were the 'people of the book', as described in the holy Qur'an, they were supposed to be the first to acknowledge the message of Prophet

Mohammed. However, far from acknowledging the Prophet's message, they mocked him and rejected him. They tried to delegitimize and ridicule his call. On one occasion, the Jews of Medina cooperated with Mohammed's enemies, the pagans, in the third battle known by the name of *Al-Khandaq*, which took place between the Muslims and a coalition of the pagan Quriesh tribes who then dwelt in Mecca. The Prophet saw them as a potential threat to his rule and eventually evicted them from Medina. Subsequence mistrust and enmity led the Muslim rulers to evict the Jews completely from the Arabian Peninsula. In my own discussions with numerous Islamists in Jordan regarding peace with Israel, they consistently hold on to one argument: their conviction that negotiations with the Israelis are futile because the Jews are cunning and cannot be trusted. This line of thinking goes on and on, but the bottom line is that even if a pact with the Jews could be agreed, as the Prophet reached in the past, the Jews would spare no opportunity to exploit it to their advantage. Simply put, according to the Islamists, Jews cannot be trusted.

Seen in this light, the Islamists believed that Jews were dubbed in the Qur'an as "the most hostile in intent toward the believers". They were only matched, in their enmity, by the pagans whom Prophet Mohammed waged a series of wars against to force them to accept his call of monotheism. The arsenal within the ideological baggage of the Islamist is enormous and contains a large number of attributes that early Muslims ascribe to the Jews during their bitter confrontations. For instance, Jews during the Prophet's era were dubbed as "greedy", "cowards" and "cunning". The Qur'an itself states that the Jews betrayed the call and teaching of their prophet Moses. They were seen as the most vehement in their enmity to the believers. To substantiate their belief that the Jews are cunning, the Islamists often invoked the incident where the Jews made a pact with the Prophet only to turn against him by allying themselves with the pagans – the same pagans who tried to finish him off in one of the battles that Mohammed eventually prevailed in. Much has been said and written on the experience, interaction and confrontation between the Jews and Prophet Mohammed during the latter's rule in Medina. From the beginning, it was never an easy relationship.

For many Muslims nowadays, the bitter experience the Prophet had with the Jews has informed much of their perception of Israel today. This vision, or collective memory, has shaped the way the Arabs, and indeed the Muslims, view Israel and has become the prism through which they conceptualize the Jews and Israel. Islamic movements on the whole have a strong intellectual and theological link to this memory. It is from this long memory that political and religious concepts emanate. Islamists monopolize this narrative and prevent any effort to reinterpret this period. In my readings, I have not encountered any alternative interpretation of this era that is substantially different from that of the Islamists. The ultimate objective has remained to expel the Jews from Palestine. An often-reiterated slogan in demonstrations is "Khaybar, Khaybar oh ye Jews, Mohammed's army will come back".[16]

Central to this perspective is the Islamic religious foundation that derives much of its content from verses from the Holy Qur'an. Images of Jews are projected based on stories included in the Holy Qur'an. The stereotypical qualities of the Jews reported in the Qur'an during the Prophet's dealing with them are often invoked to depict, analyze and understand Israeli policies and moves in the region. The interaction and conflict between Muslims and Jews in the early days of the Islamic call constitutes the historical and intellectual framework on which Islamists base their understanding of modern Israel.[17]

Some Islamic movements, such as Hamas and Hezbollah, are also motivated by the national consideration, which adds another layer to their perspective. They view Israel within the national perspective that sees Israel as a settlers' entity that has been established at the expense of the Palestinians and supported by great powers. Here, the similarity between the Islamists' ideology and the pan-Arabist one is striking. However, the religious constituent of political Islam is the dominant one, so Jews continue to be viewed primarily from a religious, Islamic perspective. The solution is to establish a Palestinian state in all of historical Palestine that would cancel the Jewish or Zionist nature of the state. To some extent, the secular Palestinian movement called for the same end in the 1970s when it espoused the secular Palestinian state.

By far the most conspicuous theme in this perspective is the confidence that Israel is a temporary entity that will not stand on its own as time goes by. Islamists often invoke the existence of crusaders in Palestine as telling evidence that foreign entities on Arab and Muslim land will vanish one day. Against this background, the solution is that Israel is a temporary entity and liberation of Palestinian territories from the Mediterranean to the Jordan River is the ultimate solution that will put an end to the Jewish and Zionist nature of the state and replace it with an Arab–Islamic one. However, some other forces such as Hamas are suggesting some kind of phased solution.

In an attempt to stress the idea that Israel will perish, Kamal Mohammed al-Astal wrote a book comparing the crusaders to the Zionists and explicitly predicting the disappearance of Israel.[18] The main idea of this book is derived from the inevitability syndrome: Israel is going to vanish regardless of the material condition or the prevailing balance of power in the region. He makes the case that there are many regional similarities between the crusader invasion and the Zionist settler colonization example in Palestine. Firstly, both of them represent foreign presence in the region, as both belong to Western civilization and each of them is a spearhead for that civilization in a confrontation with Asian civilization. He also argues that the internal qualities of both structures are similar. The internal qualities that put an end to the crusaders will ultimately put an end to the Zionist presence.[19] In the book, al-Astal compares the first crusader king with Ben-Gurion and also makes comparisons between the crusader Prince of Kerek and Moshe Dayan by suggesting that both were reckless.

In his conclusion, al-Astal predicts the form of conflict in the first quarter of the twenty-first century. He comes up with a formula: Muslim society against the Jewish Zionist entity = elimination of, or melting of, the entity.[20] He assures us that there will be no other alternative to this scenario. He makes the case that Israeli success is both formal and temporary and time is working against Israel. Indeed, many Islamists attach no value to time. They can wait indefinitely, categorizing the conflict as a historical one. What is crucial is that, according to the Islamists, the ultimate victory will be theirs. In addition, al-Astal stresses the pan-Arab level of the conflict. In his words: "Israel is in fact an artificial entity. Although it tries to derive sources for its regional power, the survival of Israel as a Zionist state and as a manifestation of political Zionism is contingent upon what function Israel can fulfill for the global powers that dominate or will dominate the international system in the future."[21] Al-Astal defines a number of functions for Israel, and warns that failure to meet these functions will lead to its disappearance. The first function is that Israel is a supporting tool to forces hostile to Arab unity. According to this line of thinking, it is in the best interests of the great powers to see the region fragmented and Israel can play a role in this. The second function is for Israel to be a contact link between European civilization and the Arab region. This means Israel must continue protecting the political interests of the West in the region. The third function that al-Astal lists, is for Israel to be a tool to defend American strategy in the Indian Ocean. Finally, Israel must be an outpost for world imperialism and for the multinational corporations.[22] The author is certain that Israel will not be able to implement these changes in the future and for this reason it is going to disappear in the coming years. Furthermore, rather than viewing internal differences as a strengthening factor, al-Astal views them as a weakness capable of eroding Israeli society. In fact, diversity and pluralism can be a factor of strength especially in a democratic society. It is worth quoting his final two paragraphs,

> It could be said that the international framework is working against the future of Israel, as did the regional framework. Arab unity is going to materialize and will surround Israel in direct relations. The pan-Arab framework is working against Israel as well. As Israel suffers from internal problems and will not be able to carry out its job for the contending great powers within

the next thirty years, Israel will not be able to continue in existence as an international force.[23]

This inevitability syndrome was reflected in another book by Abdelwahab Elmessiri entitled *Inhiyar Israel Min 'Dakhil* (Collapse of Israel from Within).[24] To start with, the book lacks any consistency or link among its chapters. Indeed Elmessiri only addresses the main question of his inquiry in the seventh chapter. This chapter is based on wishful analysis to say the least. The author fails to build a solid case to justify his claim that Israel is going to disappear due to internal factors. He briefly touches on the phenomenon of soldiers defecting from the army. While defection of soldiers is happening all the time in Israel, he insinuates that this is as an indication of Israel's eventual or even imminent downfall. His argument is that defection is a dangerous matter in a settler pocket that is tasked to fight by its patrons.[25] He cites one defector who was freed from prison as saying,

> I was fully confident that I had condemned myself to social excommunication because of my refusal to serve in the army. But Israeli society has changed rapidly during the last five years. Stigmatizing those who refuse to serve in the army no longer exists. I feel that the sacred view of the army has disappeared. Also, those who remain fond of the army understand my ideology and understand that they join the army because they believe in it and I don't because I don't believe in service.[26]

Elmessiri argues that many Israeli youths realize that the Zionist state does not just defend itself but is an aggressive state and cite the 1982 invasion of Lebanon as an example.[27]

The youths Elmessiri interviewed believed that their country's invasion was wrong. While the presentation of his examples is well documented and indeed correct, Elmessiri tends to read too much into these separate incidents leading him to overreach in his conclusions. His linkage example that the collapse of Israel is imminent due to the collapse of the national consensus is not convincing. Opinion polls have shown consistently that Israelis have always felt that their personal and national security was threatened. He includes some selective quotes but ignores all polls and scientific studies that contradict what he wants the reader to believe. By his final chapter, he has failed to show how Israel is going to collapse from within. Apparently, he thinks that his argument will be taken for granted by the Arab readership given their animosity towards Israel, and thus vindicates his position with a few unconvincing examples.

At the end of the chapter he raises the question of whether Israel is going to collapse from within due to "acute crisis and internal contradiction"? He goes on to list the factors that weaken Israel. They range from the retreat of the Kibbutz movement, to drugs, gays, the erosion of families in Israel and violence among school students. It is worth mentioning that by including the existence of the gay community within the factors of weakness, he and all the Islamists pass moral judgment against gays. He sees the existence of gays and their actions simply as a sin. He also states: "perhaps the acceptance of the Israeli society of homosexuality is manifested in the number of lesbians who gave birth… and this may be because of the attempt by the settler pocket to bypass its demographic crisis."[28] Despite his encyclopedic knowledge of Israel, Elmessiri fails to see pluralism and diversity as a source of resilience for any democratic society. It is ironic that although Elmessiri spends the entire book laying the ground for reasons why the state of Israel is on the verge of collapse, by his concluding chapter he asserts that after reviewing of all the destructive components of Israeli society, he cannot see an imminent collapse. This is a surprising and an abrupt conclusion given the tone of the book. He has used the argument that life in the 'Zionist gathering' is not derived from within but from without as it is aided financially, military and politically by the United States, the Western world and the Jewish communities and therefore it is not going to collapse from within. He claims that finishing off this settler pocket is not possible without ongoing daily *jihad* against it. His conclusion, that only by ongoing *jihad* will Israel come to an end, shows how firmly he is influenced by the Islamist discourse. He goes on to argue that factors of societal erosion can be employed in the Arab and Muslim favor and demonstrate the limit of our enemy and that it is not a big, invincible force. In the last line of the book, Elmessiri underscores the importance of *jihad* against the enemy. To sum up, as the conclusion of the book does not follow logically from the text it is therefore scholarship that is loaded with wishful thinking.

Although Elmessiri adopts the functional role theory of Israel as explained in the previous chapter, he also buys into the Islamists' linchpin argument; that Israel will vanish. This ideological illusion is reflected in his writings. In his words, the Israeli entity is a weak one that has emerged among Arab countries and its survival until now is an indication of the Arab *takhadul* (hesitation and weakness) and not proof of Israeli prowess. In an online interview he says: "the Jews of the world are refusing to go to Israel because the Intifada has sent a message that Israelis are liars, and that this state that claims that it is Jewish has failed until now to define Judaism and the existence of contradiction between what is religious and what is secular".[29] To him these are indications of the possible demise of Israel because life in the Zionist state gains its resources not from within but relies on outside, mainly American, support.

The inability of writers to see the changing reality is a function of a closed belief system that tends to hang on to certain concepts and discourses. For instance, Ali Miss'ad Taha Faraj published a book entitled *Israel: Where to?!* This book is a study of the thoughts and history of the Jews and the destiny of their current country Israel. In the fifth chapter, the author suggests Qur'anic and material evidence that proves Israel's eventual disappearance. For instance, he mentions the following verse from the Qur'an:

> And we gave (clear) warning to the Children of Israel in the Book, that twice would they do mischief on the earth and be elated with mighty arrogance (and twice would they be punished)! [5] When the first of the warnings came to pass, We sent against you Our servants given to terrible warfare. They entered the very inmost parts of your homes; and it was a warning (completely) fulfilled. [6] Then did we grant you the Return as against them: We gave you increase in resources and sons, and made you the more numerous in man-power. [7] If ye did well, ye did well for yourselves; if ye did evil, (ye did it) against yourselves. So when the second of the warnings came to pass, (We permitted your enemies) to disfigure your faces, and to enter your Temple as they had entered it before, and to visit with destruction all that fell into their power.[30]

This verse refers to what is included in the Qur'an as the corruption of the Jews on earth for a second time. He argues that the message in the Qur'an is directed at those who believe in it and to ensure that they benefit from it. This is to direct the Muslims' attention towards what the Jews will be like, for instance in their plotting against Islam, while also assuring the believers that the final confrontation will be in Muslims' favor after, God willing, they manage to defeat the enemies who are gathering in Palestine. He also refers to the Prophet's statement that the Day of Judgment will not come before the Muslims fight the Jews. "The Muslims will kill the Jews who will hide behind rocks and trees and later the Muslims will be called to come and kill the Jews hiding behind the rocks."[31]

The author also touches upon material conditions that will accelerate the disappearance of Israel. Of all the indicators, the divisions that the "Zionist entity is suffering from in Palestine" is the author's most telling evidence of the arguments that Israel will eventually disappear. The author considers Israel illegitimate and therefore concludes that it would be impossible for Israel to integrate into the region simply because Israel is a colonizing state that usurped land that did not belong to it. Seen from this perspective, the author makes the case that Israeli society will remain alien in the land that it inhabits.[32] Furthermore, from the author's perspective, what is more troubling for Israel, is the small country's lack of natural resources and its dependence on external aid.[33]

Conclusion

In this chapter, I have provided and discussed a few texts that I believe are representative of books that are greatly informed by the Islamist discourse. Evidently, Islamic movements in the Arab world have held the hegemonic discourse on Israel for an extended period of time. This religious discourse has contributed, in no small amount, to setting the tone for debate over Israel and what should be done in regard to it. Hence, their attitude towards Israel and the Zionists is of critical importance. If anything, writing on Israel has become a means of proving the vulnerability of the Zionist entity, while re-emphasizing its ultimate destiny, which is to vanish. For this reason, few studies have tackled Israel from within, and in the instances where they did, the impact of the Arab–Israeli conflict and the hegemonic discourse have informed much of the analysis.

Strikingly, much of the writing on Israel is informed by the interpretation that stems from this hegemonic perspective. The jargon dates back to the early experience of the Prophet Mohammed with the Jews. The negative stereotypes of the Jewish community during the time of the Prophet were often invoked to describe modern Israel. Even if Israel, for example, was genuine about peace as was the case with the Rabin government, Islamists quickly invoke the 'cunning and deceitful' attributes that are mentioned in the Qur'an as a timeless attestation of truth. Jews are projected in the Qur'an as rejecting the truth of God, and having no respect for their own prophets. For this reason, Islamists tend to show a closed belief system that discards any new information that clashes with their already existing set of stereotypical images of the Jews.

These characteristics are collectively seen by Islamists as the driving force behind the Israelis' relentless plotting and conspiring against the Muslims and the Arabs. A recurrent theme in their writing is that Israelis plot with imperial powers to split the Muslim world, thus enabling Israel to triumph. Even 'establishment Islam' sees Israel in a similar way. A few years before the Camp David accords, leading clergymen of al-Azhar such as Shaikh Ali Jadd al-Haqq had voiced similar sentiments.

Notes

1   He was a Syrian intellectual who belonged to the Islamic modernism tradition. His writing focused on the relative weakness of Muslim societies compared to the West. He looked inward to answer the question as to why the Muslims failed to achieve advances in science and technology.

2   *Al-Manar*, vol. 33, part 4, June 1933, p. 273.

3   The public atmosphere was tense in 1930s as Palestinian leader, Amin Husseini, known as the grand mufti, led the Palestinian revolution from 1936–39.

4   Hassan al-Banna, *Mudhakarat Al-Da'wa Wi Da'iya* (Memories of the Call and the Caller) (Cairo: Dar El-Shihab).

5   Sayyid Qutb, *Ma'alim fi al-Tariq* (Milestones) (Cairo: Dar al-Elshuruq, 1970).

6   For a discussion of this issue see Maha Azzam, "Islamism Revisited", *International Affairs*, vol. 82, no. 6 (2006), p. 1130.

7   Nathan Brown, Amr Hamzawy, and Marina Ottaway, "Islamist Movements and the Democratic Process in the Arab World: Exploring Gray Zones", *Carnegie Paper*, no. 67 (March 2006).

8   Mohammed Abd al-Salam Faraj, "The Absent Duty", in Rifaat Sayed Ahmed (ed.), *The Militant Prophet: The Revolutionaries,* vol. 2 (London: Riad El-Rayyes Books, 1991), pp. 137–49.

9   Mohammed Abd al-Salam Faraj, "The Absent Duty".

10 For the shift from local to global jihad see Fawaz A. Gerges, *The Far Enemy: Why Jihad Went Global* (New York: Cambridge University Press, 2005).

11 See issues of *al-Sabeel*, a weekly published by the Islamic Action Front (the political wing of the Muslim Brotherhood) in Jordan. See issues especially during al-Aqsa Intifada.

12 For details on Jordanian anti-normalization activities, see Hassan A. Barari, *Jordan and Israel: Ten Years Later* (Amman: CSS, 2004), pp. 43–58.

13 For a good discussion of the Jihadi movements, see Fawaz A. Gerges, *The Far Enemy.*

14 www.washington-report.org (Accessed 2 October 2007).

15 Saad Eddin Ibrahim, "Domestic Developments in Egypt", in William Quandt (ed.), *The Middle East: Ten Years After Camp David* (Washington, DC: Brookings Institution, 1988), p. 53.

16 This is a slogan that is oft-reiterated in demonstrations organized by the Islamists in different Arab countries. In the year 629 Muhammad and his followers attacked the Jews living in the oasis of Khaybar, located 150 kilometers from Medina. The Muslims attacked Jews who, having reached agreement with the Muslims and then broken their word, had barricaded themselves in a fort. The Jews were defeated and surrendered, but were allowed to continue living in the oasis on the condition that they gave one-half of their produce to the Muslims. Jews continued to live in the oasis for several more years until they were finally expelled by Caliph Omar.

17 Dia Raswhan, "Dia, Ru'a Al-'islam Al-Haraki" (Visions of Activist Islam), in Center for Political Research and Studies, *Egyptian Visions of Israel* (Cairo: Cairo University, 2002), pp. 57–62.

18 Kamal Mohammed al-Astal, *Mustaqbal Israel Bayn Al-'Sti'sal wat Tadweeb* (The Future of Israel Between Elimination and Assimilation) (Dar 'Lmawqif Al-'Arabi, 1980).

19 *Ibid.*, pp. 10–11.

20 *Ibid.*, p. 274.

21 *Ibid.*, p. 284.

22 *Ibid.*, p. 284.

23 *Ibid.*, p. 287.

24 Abdelwahab Elmessiri, *Inhiyar Israel Min 'Dakhil* (Collapse of Israel from Within) (Cairo: Dar 'lma'arif, 2001).

25 *Ibid.*, p. 161.

26 *Ibid.*, p. 162.

27 *Ibid.*, p. 165.

28 *Ibid.*, pp. 181–2.

29 www.arabiyat.com/magazine/publisher, 5 October 2006.

30 Ali Miss'ad Taha Faraj, *Israel, 'La 'Ayn?!: Dirasah Fi Fikr Wa Tarikh Al-Yahud Wa Massir Dawlatuhum 'Lhaliya* (Israel, Where to?!: A Study in the Thinking and History of the Jews and the Destiny of their Current State, 1999) (Cairo: Ein For Human and Social Studies, 1999), p. 145.

31 *Ibid.*, p. 153.

32 *Ibid.*, p. 154.

33 *Ibid.*, p. 157.

4

Arab Regimes and the Making
of a Discourse

——

*Colonialism has tried all means to emasculate our Arabism and to
drive a wedge among us. Therefore, the creation of Israel came
as a product of colonialism.*

Nasser, 26 July 1956

*If I were an Arab leader, I would never accept the existence of Israel. This is
only natural. We took their land. True, God promised it to us, but what does it
matter to them? There was anti-Semitism, the Nazis, Hitler, Auschwitz, but was
it their fault? They only see one thing: we came and took their land. They may
forget in a generation or two, but for the time being there is no choice.*

David Ben-Gurion, the first Israeli Prime Minster

*So leave our land
Our shores, our sea
Our Wheat, our salt, our wound*

Mahmoud Darwish[1]

Introduction

In the previous chapters, a link was firmly established between one's own perspective or ideology and the process of interpreting the theme under study, which then underpins the hegemony of a discourse. This linkage is apparent in much of the Arab scholarship on Israel. In this chapter, I will discuss the significance of the official (regime) discourse and its impact on the way authors saw Israel over past decades. However, one cannot make the case that there has been a single official discourse that reflects the perspectives of all regimes. Arab regimes have been divided along political and ideological lines for much of the post-1948 war period.[2] Hence, the regime's discourses have not only been dissimilar, but have even gone as far as adopting opposition discourses, including Islamic and secular ones.

Central to this chapter is the argument that the Arab regimes have persistently used the Arab–Israeli conflict and played up anti-Israel statements to deflect attention from their domestic problems and the demand that they embark on genuine reform that would render the regimes powerless vis-à-vis their people. Time and again, Arab regimes have focused on the external challenge, namely Israel, as an effective tool for shaping and manipulating internal political and socio-economic conditions in the interest of their political survival. The result has been irresistible hegemonic discourse that has affected the impartiality of scholars and pundits and conditioned much of the way they have written on Israel. An example of one tactic employed by the regimes was when Jordan devalued its currency in 1988 as a response to what appeared to be the imminent collapse of the economy. Many senior officials pushed the fear button and accused Israel of being responsible for the state of affairs. Implicit in these statements was the aim of calming people down and reminding them of the real and authentic threat to the country. Here again, Israel was used as a tool to distract people's attention from corrupt governments and their disastrous economic policies.

Additionally, some Arab regimes believe that their relative influence, prestige and status within the inter-Arab context were derived from their firm rhetorical stands against Israel. This trend can be observed at many of the Arab League summits, with Arab leaders taking it upon themselves to grandstand and in some cases point the finger at their rivals. Bombastic statements slamming Israel have been a first-class tactic to ameliorate the regimes' images within, and among, the Arab masses. But despite the circus these statements created, few results materialized. Saddam Hussein's threat in 1990 to burn half of Israel is a case in point. His often-reiterated statements were meant to electrify the Arab masses and they indeed succeeded. He consistently underscored the looming danger of Israel and the ability of Iraq to chip away at this potent threat. He managed to persuade the Arab masses, who saw Israel as an aggressor, of the efficacy of using force against Israel. Paradoxically, he ended up invading Kuwait instead of 'liberating' Palestine. In a last ditch attempt to solicit the Arab masses' support for this war of aggrandizement, he ordered the firing of 39 missiles against Israel during the war with the American-led coalition in mid-January 1991. Despite his stinging defeat in the war, Saddam enjoyed a remarkable popularity in much of the Arab world simply because of what appeared to be firm stands against Israel and America.

The political manipulation of the conflict on the part of Arab regimes only reinforced the stereotypes of Israel and thus accentuated the popular animosity towards it. Ironically, when Arab regimes have signed peace treaties with Israel, they have been unaware of their contribution to the level of entrenched and deep-seated anti-Israeli sentiments. As a consequence, their efforts to enlist support for the imperatives of their new foreign policy vis-à-vis Israel suffered from two interrelated problems. Firstly, people continued to find it hard to get over the impact of the dominant discourse that the regimes themselves contributed to. Secondly, the public's perceptions had been informed by the continuation of the conflict and what they saw as Israel's relentless attempt to hold on to Palestinian land and to consolidate its expansion at the expense of the Palestinian people.

The Role of Israel: Exploiting the Conflict

To the chagrin of Arab nationalists, not only was the state of Israel established in 1948, but it also managed to prevail in the war. The Arabs' defeat produced hundreds of thousands of Palestinian refugees.[3] Arabs dub the war as the *nakba* (catastrophe) and have not reconciled themselves with the new emerging strategic environment. In the first two decades following the war, Israel successfully nipped in the bud all Arab attempts to build up any force that might reverse or undo the outcome of 1948.

Evidently, one of the far-reaching consequences of the war was the widespread feeling of disgrace among the Arabs and the discredit of regimes that had failed to muster enough force to fight and defeat what had been seen as a vulnerable Jewish *Yishuv* (Jewish community in Palestine).[4] On the whole, Arabs did not understand how it was possible for Israel to prevail when it was fought by a combination of many Arab countries. Time and again, Sati al-Husri was asked to provide an explanation for the defeat of seven Arab states at the hand of one state. His answer was that they had lost precisely because they were seven states.[5] The message that he was trying to drive home was that the Arabs comprised one nation and should therefore be united in one state – only then would the Arab world be formidable. Al-Husri and like-minded intellectuals were not happy with the fact that the Arabs were fragmented into several weak and artificial countries. The Arab state system, which was largely created and shaped by colonial powers (mainly Britain and France), came into being after the end of the First World War. It was this very system that they sought to transform.

The catastrophe of 1948 continually reminded the Arabs of their impotence as long as they were divided. Therefore, Arab revolutionary regimes (chief among them, of course, Nasser of Egypt) focused on the issue of Arab unity as a means to achieve strength and emancipation.[6] Initially, Nasser was an Egyptian patriot who had a fixation on one issue: freezing the British out of Egypt. Notwithstanding his rhetoric against Israel, he remained focused on driving the British out of Egypt. When the former US Secretary of State, John Foster Dulles, tried to recruit Nasser to support a defensive alliance against the Soviets in 1953, Nasser was not moved. He reminded Dulles that the Soviets were more than five thousand miles away from Egypt, and that the British presence in Egypt was the main threat.

Nasser's position was that the number one enemy for Egypt and the region was Western colonization.[7] Israel, in Nasser's thinking, was nothing but an integral part and a tool of colonization planted in the region to destabilize it and to emasculate pan-Arabism. Nasser's obsession with imperialism prevented him from seeing things in anything other than binary ways. For instance, he placed 'reactionary' regimes (particularly Jordan and Saudi Arabia) on a par with Israel considering them to be tools in the hands of the colonizers. He argued that these reactionary regimes were linked to colonization and to Israel, in an attempt to put an end to the 'progressive' regimes. His belief system on the Arab–Israeli conflict and the role of imperialism and Arab reactionaries was part of a collective Arab pan-Arabist belief system.

Whether Nasser was sincere about the notion of unity or not, he discovered that pan-Arabism was a powerful tool for defending Egypt's interests in the region and for bestowing a domestic legitimacy on him. Realizing that he would not be able to withstand Western influence in the region, Nasser resorted to pan-Arabism as a potent tool to make the most of the Arabs' anti-imperialist sentiments.[8] Pan-Arabism furnished Nasser's propaganda at a time when Egyptian nationalism furnished his behaviors. It was invoked to justify Nasser's interference in Lebanon, Jordan and Iraq to forestall these countries from allying themselves with the Western powers encircling Syria and to help him remove all vestiges of foreign control.

Undoubtedly, the rhetoric of pan-Arabism that was injected into the people electrified the Arab masses, particularly in the Meshreq, and posed a credible menace to the stability of other regimes such as Jordan. In other words, pan-Arabism threatened many other regimes and instead of uniting the Arabs it actually led, ironically, to the division of the Arab world into two camps vying for influence in a very volatile region. As Malcolm Kerr succinctly put it: "the enemies of Arabism were held to be the 'reactionaries' – hereditary monarchs, oligarchic politicians, and wealthy landowners and businessmen – who found it easier to obstruct reforms by keeping the Arab world divided. Their alleged cooperation with the imperialists was held to be simply a facet of their reactionary outlook."[9] With the advent of the unity between Egypt and Syria in 1958, the Arab Cold War between the two camps came to the fore. As a corollary, pan-Arabism was employed by the self-proclaimed 'progressive' regimes, such as Egypt and Syria, in their bid for regional hegemony. Pan-Arabism questioned the existence of so many Arab states as an artificial creation of the colonial powers. Therefore, hostility towards imperial or Western influence in the region and Israel remained an outstanding tenet in the ideology of pan-Arabism.

Against this backdrop, Arab regimes were in a race to see who could adopt the firmest and most assertive rhetoric towards Israel, the offspring of imperialism. The Arabs' obsession with the Palestinians' cause stemmed from the widely held conviction that Israel had been implanted, despite the wishes of the Arabs, by the colonial powers, particularly Britain. The existence of refugees in Egypt, Jordan, Syria and Lebanon was a constant reminder to the Arabs of their powerlessness. Therefore championing the Palestinian cause was one of the rallying cards in inter-Arab politics. On the whole, countries used the conflict as a tool to boost their regimes' internal legitimacy and to cast doubt on the legitimacy of their opponents, whether states or political forces, within each country.

At the heart of inter-Arab politics lay the problem of legitimacy that was an integral part of the Arab state system following its creation in the wake of the First World War and the eclipse of the Ottoman Empire. The legitimacy problem has been a chronic symptom of the Arab state system particularly in the Fertile Crescent (Iraq, Syria, Jordan, Lebanon and Palestine). The borders of the new Arab states were drawn by the colonial powers in arbitrary ways and failed to take account of the already existing social, ethnic and economical links between the different people who came under the new concept of sovereignty. Far from helping achieve Arab unity, the colonial powers (Britain and France) plotted against the Arabs' aspiration for self-determination in the infamous Sykes-Picot Agreement of 1916 that divided the Arab world into spheres of influence. More troubling was the fact that the new states were ruled by elites that were mainly installed by the colonial powers, a dimension that further complicated the issue of legitimacy. To a large extent, the foreign policy of Arab countries was controlled by colonial powers. Jordan, for instance, never had a foreign policy of its own until the independence of the country in 1946. Before that, its foreign policy had been the colonial one. This state of affairs contributed, in no small part, to the legitimacy deficit that many Arab regimes have suffered from then up until the present day.

In their quest for political legitimacy, Arab regimes have had to address the inherent clash between Arab nationalism and state nationalism that has made the Arab state system such a unique phenomenon. The key challenge has been to square the various conflicting interests of the state with the tutelage of Arab nationalism. Each state has a different socio-economic system with different natural resources that have dictated different foreign policies. As one would expect, the ruling elites in all countries have placed their state's interests ahead of collective pan-Arabist ideals. Additionally, the ruling elites of all countries alike feared unity lest this deprive them of the vested interests which they enjoyed in the current state of disunity. Worse still, it is hard to point to any regime that was elected by the people. As Michael Hudson succinctly puts it: "the central problem of government in the Arab world today is political legitimacy. The shortage of this indispensable political resource largely accounts for the volatile nature of Arab politics and the autocratic, unstable character of all the present Arab governments."[10]

Ironically, repression, assassination and military coups d'état become rational behaviors given the legitimacy deficit. Some national and revolutionary regimes preached policies that proved detrimental to the Arab cause in the long run. These policies included liberation of the entire land of historic Palestine, staving off all kinds of external intervention in the region, and the realization of a sort of Arab solidarity if not unity.[11]

In their search for national legitimacy, Arab regimes, without exception, look to external sources for this rather rare commodity. Undoubtedly, the best source of legitimacy, and indeed the Arab core concern, is the issue of Palestine and the need to stand up to the Zionists. Arab leaders have attached great importance to appearing as though they were taking a stand against the Israeli threat. The lack of legitimacy created a strategic environment that made these countries susceptible to external penetration and internal pressures. The conflict with Israel gave these Arab regimes the weapon to pre-empt subversive external, as well as internal, threats. In other words, the exploitation of the Palestinian cause "served as a stopgap, legitimacy-rich mechanism to compensate for their poor legitimacy at home, inter-state divisions, and failure to materialize the masses' social and economic expectations."[12]

If anything, the dialectic between state nationalism and trans-state nationalism (pan-Arabism) and the search for legitimacy led to the ascendance of autocratic states in the Arab world. Israel was used to account for much of the internal failures, thus reminding us of George Orwell's novel, *Animal Farm*, in which an external enemy was created, or over-exaggerated, to keep internal differences at bay. This also involved a different kind of repression, which in turn compromised political and academic freedom. As a corollary, scholars found it really hard to think out of the box already created by the hegemonic discourses. We now turn to the lack of academic and political freedom in the Arab world as a key reason for the underdevelopment of Israeli studies. Each Arab country censored scholarship, and the lack of academic freedom has crippled social sciences, particularly in relation to Israel.

Political and Academic Freedom

It is not unnatural to argue that the lack of political and academic freedom in the Arab world stems from the fact that most of the Arabs live under repressive and authoritarian regimes. Amazingly, the Arab world has defied the proliferation of elected governments across the world. Rarely if at all in the Arab world has a president or a king been replaced through the ballot box. A Freedom House Annual Report suggests that none of the 121 countries in the world that are deemed electoral democracies are Arab.[13] Despite the democratization process that has characterized a few states in the Arab world recently, the fact remains that genuine democracy has yet to take root. Reasons for this state of affairs abound and a quick review of the literature on authoritarianism and the democratic deficit in the Arab world reveals two main schools of thought that tackle this burning topic: the political–cultural and the political–economic schools of thought.

The political–cultural approach attributes the lack of democracy or freedom in the Arab world to the Islamic/Arab culture. Bernard Lewis, for instance, blames it on Islam. He argues that the history of the Middle East, especially under the rule of the caliphs, is a main reason for the lack of participatory governance. He argues that citizens' obedience to the ruler was a religious duty and therefore disobedience was seen as a sin.[14] The predominance of the patriarchal system, patrimonial leadership, kinship, tribes, primordialism and the emphasis on God have contributed, to some extent, to the current stagnation especially with regards to democracy, liberty and freedom. While there is an element of truth in this argument, this Orientalist approach, to put it mildly, fails to capture the intricacies of the dynamics of Arab and Islamic societies. It simply fails to account for the fact that some Islamic countries, such as Turkey and Indonesia, have managed to have participatory governments despite being Muslim countries. Therefore, the argument that Islam impedes democracy is not only a lopsided one but it also does not stand up to empirical evidence. Lisa Anderson rightly attacks this 'Orientalist' approach and considers it to be too ethnocentric, deterministic and teleological.[15]

The second approach is the political–economic one. This is, in my opinion, more robust than the former as it examines the interplay between economics and politics. In his book, *Overstating the Arab State*, Nazih Ayubi makes the case that authoritarianism took root in the Arab world because of, to use the Marxist parlance, the Asiatic mode of production.[16] In addition, Arab societies are characterized as having a fluid class structure that has contributed, to some extent, to the lack of participatory political institutions. This is a result of the state's profound involvement in economic affairs. Others, like Hazem Beblawi, employ the rentierism theory to account for the lack of democracy in the Gulf Arab states. A key string of this discourse is that the state extracts wealth from oil and redistributes it to the people. Governments do not tax people and as a quid pro quo, people show no interest in democracy.[17] Indeed, citizens are not part of the production but rather are dependent, either directly or indirectly, on governmental expenditures. Petrodollars are recycled to poorer non-oil Arab states such as Jordan. This is done through remittance from workers in the Gulf. The argument is that this recycling generates similar, though not identical, political dynamics in the countries that receive work remittance. Some Arab countries rely on strategic rent accrued directly from foreign aid, debt write-offs and easy loans, thus making the state less dependent on its citizens.

Each of the two approaches provides important insights into the dynamic of authoritarianism and democratic deficit, yet neither of them is able to provide a sufficient explanation to account for chronic political stagnation in the Arab world. Therefore, to fully account for the continuation of autocracy, these two trends of analysis need to be complemented by another one, namely the link between the continuation of the Arab–Israeli conflict and the unwillingness of the Arab regimes to allow democracy to take root. Simply put, the Arab regimes use the conflict as an excuse for not embarking on genuine reform and democracy. Thus, the role of foreign policy as a tool or an excuse to perpetuate autocracy and lack of genuine democracy should not be downplayed. Seen from this perspective, the existence of Israel and the continuation of the Arab–Israeli conflict has been used to bestow legitimacy on the Arab regimes, especially by the Arab countries that surround Israel.

Evidently, and as the discussion below will illustrate, Israel is invoked repeatedly as Arab regimes try to stifle domestic resentment and to perpetuate autocratic rule.[18] In many Arab countries, it is not possible to publish a book before receiving the permission of a governmental agency, with all the censorship that involves. Many scholars have been jailed because they have criticized their regime. An example of this was the prominent Egyptian sociologist, Saad Eddin Ibrahim, who was jailed in Egypt because he dared to criticize the idea of inherited presidency. Arab jails are full of writers who think and write outside the box especially on internal issues. Therefore, surviving and keeping one's career entails compliance with the mainstream discourse.

The press department in many Arab countries censors every written publication to make sure that it does not embarrass the regime. Freedom of expression, and even freedom of association, is limited. This is obvious especially in the media. According to the Arab Human Development Report of 2002, only three Arab countries (Lebanon, Egypt and Jordan) have partly free media.[19] For this reason, objective writing has frequently fallen victim to censorship.

Even translation from Hebrew into Arabic has suffered the same fate. Ghazi Sa'di, the founder and director of a research center in Jordan who has translated many books from Hebrew into Arabic, argues that translation requires us to tone down and in many cases to change the text. One of the books Sa'di translated is a book written by a prominent Israeli scholar, Asher Susser, on the Jordanian Prime Minister Wasfi Tell.[20] Sa'di had to omit two chapters and even then the translated book never saw the light because of censorship.[21]

The lack of political and academic freedom and the existence of repressive authoritarian regimes, coupled with the perpetuation of the Arab–Israeli conflict, have informed writing on Israel. It has been influenced by politics and the need to make polemical rather than academic points. For this reason, Arab scholars have not yet managed to match their Israeli counterparts in challenging the official and ideological narratives of the Arab regimes as the New Historians did in Israel. In other words, there simply is no revisionist Arab school of thought. It is striking how the interpretations of Israel's New Historians are played-up by the media and used in the Arab world as further proof of their righteous and factual positions. Indeed, there has been a tendency to dismiss as *a priori* any notion that does not fit neatly within their already established perspective. Obviously, this is a function of the closed-belief system that I referred to earlier in the book.

A close look at Arab historiography on the most important interaction with Israel (the 1948 war) reveals a rather stark story. Much of the writing is non-scholarly. It relies much on collective memories and much less on critical scrutiny of the era or event.[22] This situation has not changed much for two reasons. Firstly, the continuation of the Arab–Israeli conflict, which has made the Arabs more obsessed with scoring points against Israel in their bid to win over international opinion. Secondly, Arab regimes have yet to allow researchers to use the archives of this era. Even six decades after 1948 and the death of all Arab leaders involved in the war, the archives remain inaccessible. For these reasons, scholars have to rely either on their collective memory or on documents available in Britain. Logistical constraints prevent them from having access to Israeli documents. Needless to say, the latter would be dismissed in any case, especially if they did not fit into the already existing collective mindset.

Arab historiography of the 1948 war was used to boost the legitimacy of the regimes as a means of propaganda campaign against other rival Arab regimes. Therefore, it is marred by the existence of a plethora of versions and full of accusations and recriminations in an attempt to find a scapegoat for the *nakba*. This is the case because the war in 1948 left deep scars on the collective Arab conscience. It will suffice to look briefly at Jordanian historiography to drive home this point. The Jordanian army entered the war and managed to secure the West Bank and East Jerusalem which would have otherwise inevitably fallen into Israeli hands. Although the Arabs were defeated in the war, the Jordanian army was the only one that could claim success by taking and defending Jerusalem at a time when the rest of the Arab armies were soundly defeated. Yet, the King of Jordan was widely accused of treason for collaboration with the Israelis. The Arabs lay at King Abdullah's door the accusation that he had been complicit in the fall of Lydda and Ramle, two Palestinian towns with more than 70,000 inhabitants who were kicked out by the Israeli forces.[23] Arab historiography is full of stories of perceived clandestine agreements between Abdullah and the Israelis to partition Palestine. Eventually, King Abdullah paid for his role in Palestine with his life in 1951.

Two books appeared immediately after the war, written by Jordanians in order to boost the King's wounded status and enhance his legitimacy. The King himself published his memoirs, which were full of disdain towards his rivals. In this book, the King defends his policies as being based on a realistic study of the situation, as opposed to his rivals who adopted reckless and miscalculated policies. He accused his rivals of lacking statesmanship and of leading their people into disasters.[24] A different approach was offered in a book written by a Jordanian officer, Mahmud al-Russan, which aimed to downplay the role played by the British soldiers in the war, and give saliency to the role of the King and the Jordanian officers.[25] Another book was published by Abdullah al-Tell, a prominent Jordanian officer during the war, in which he accused King Abdullah of Jordan of treason and of collaborating with the Israelis. He claimed that the King was a mere stooge for Britain and his role was just to implement Britain's policies. He insists that he witnessed collusion between Abdullah and the Jews, which was the explanation of the defeat adopted by the Arabs.[26] After that other books appeared in defense of King Abdullah but it was not until the 1980s that the first well-documented and scholarly book about the role of Jordan in the war was published. The book was written by a prominent Jordanian historian, Suleiman al-Musa, in which he argues that the King based his policies on realism and that the British were a constraining factor. He denies that the King agreed with the Jews to divide Palestine.[27] Many more books appeared throughout the Arab world but none were on Israel and how it functioned internally. Instead, writing on the conflict took the form of mutual accusations among the Arabs.[28]

It is worth emphasizing at this point that the Arab consensus in rejecting Israel has ceased to exist since the war in 1967. Despite the persistence of the rhetoric, the conflict now centers on borders, not the existence of Israel. This strategic change has led to more of an interest in studying Israel from within. Still, much of the writing after 1967 has been conditioned by the hegemonic discourse of the time. Another important repercussion of the war in 1967, a war that Fouad Ajami describe as the "Waterloo of Pan-Arabism" has been the bankruptcy of pan-Arabism as a working ideology and the new legitimacy of the state border. In Fouad Ajami's words: "The boundaries of the Arab states have been around now for nearly six decades. It is not their existence which is novel, but their power and legitimacy – the power (as much as that power exists in the modern state system) to keep Pan-Arab claims at bay and effectively to claim the loyalty of those within. They are no longer as 'illusionary and permeable' as they used to be."[29] This further allowed Arab countries to pursue their narrow interests, as is the case with Egypt when it signed a separate peace treaty with Israel in 1979. Seen in this way, those countries who opposed pan-Arabism were no longer at a disadvantage.

Having said that, and despite the decline of pan-Arabism, this did not translate into an automatic change of Israel's image. Arab masses have continued to embrace a common narrative and position vis-à-vis the conflict with Israel. A key reason for this is Israel's policies in the region.

Therefore in the remaining part of this chapter, I will present what I believe is the common Arab perspective on the conflict and how this impacts Arab scholarship. I would like to point out that this is not a scholarly perspective but my own description of what I believe is a common perspective among people from across the Arab region. I have had the chance to travel extensively in the Middle East and have spoken with many people from taxi drivers to intellectuals. I was once in Oman leading an American program, and I had the chance to talk to scores of people, especially at the cafe where I used to sit and smoke some hubble bubble. Their perception of Israel is within the dominant three discourses that I have tackled in the last three chapters. Even when I came across some people with a level-headed degree of critical thinking regarding the Arab, no one I have ever seen or spoken to has cast a shred of doubt on the justice of the Palestinian cause.

Israel's Policies: Reinforcing the Hegemonic Discourse

I am aware that this perspective is subjective and many Israelis will take issue with it, but I want to remind the reader just how important the issue of perspective is when talking about Arab views on Israel. I am presenting what I believe is a dominant perspective that survives moves towards peace in the Middle East. In other words, it is a kind of collective understanding (whether right or wrong) of what happened from 1948 onwards. The Arabs are obsessed by what they consider to be the absolute justice of their cause in Palestine. It is really hard to find a bifurcation of views among them on this issue. The Arab narrative of the conflict is, on the whole, a kind of a timeless attested fact. As time has passed, it has become a kind of rigid ideology. If an Arab fails to subscribe to it, he or she is seen as playing into the hands of the enemy. Indeed, due to reasons that I explained earlier in this chapter, it remains to be seen whether a new revisionist school of thought will ever emerge in the Arab world as it did in Israel.

Against this backdrop, and this is the crucial aspect of the whole issue, Arab authors understand their role as being to expose and delegitimize Israel. It has been difficult for them to embark on an objective way of studying Israel when they see a series of wars and when they interact with Palestinians refugees scattered in Jordan, Syria, Lebanon, Egypt, the West Bank, Gaza and other countries. For them the refugee problem coupled with the lack of a peaceful solution that is both just and comprehensive, prevents them from envisioning any role for themselves other than 'knowing your enemy' and the justification of fighting.[30] The conflict has thus remained a prism through which they see and view Israel.

Notwithstanding the dissonance among Arabs, perhaps the only political issue they agree on is the centrality of the Palestinian cause to their consciences and awareness. The loss of Palestine has remained an open wound in the Arab collective consciousness. If you were to bring an Arab person from the North African region to meet another Arab from, let us say, Yemen, it would not be a great surprise if the one thing that connected them was the Palestinian cause. Palestine's symbolic centrality stems from a number of factors. Firstly, Israel was implanted into the heart of the Arab world by the colonial powers of the time. Secondly, Palestine has the third holiest site for Muslims on its soil. Thirdly, Israel has inflicted a series of defeats and humiliations on the Arabs over the last six decades of ongoing conflict. Finally, the loss of Palestine brought about the birth of the Palestinian refugee problem and the existence of dozens of refugee camps in several Arab states.[31]

The overwhelming majority of the Arabs see Israel, and by extension the Jews, through the prism of this durable conflict. Thus, nothing short of an appreciation of the profound impact of the persistence of the conflict with Israel will enable us to fully understand the continuation of the kind of Israelism scholarship under scrutiny here. Undoubtedly, the persistence of the Arab–Israeli conflict and the way Israel was created, which entailed the dispossession of hundred of thousands of Palestinians, constitutes the single most important factor in the way Arabs perceive Israel. The debate about whether or not the Palestinians became refugees because they left voluntarily, as the official Israeli narrative states, or because they were forced to leave by Israel, is irrelevant. To the Arab public, Israel was the architect of the eventual ethnic cleansing of the Palestinians between 1947–49. Despite Israel's claim to the contrary, the concept of transfer was rooted in Zionist thinking during the interwar period.[32] The scattering of Palestinians to refugee camps in several Arab countries is a reminder of what the Arabs insist is an Israeli scheme of transfer. Arabs often invoke the massacre of Deir Yassin as a classic example of a Zionist scheme to empty the land of its indigenous Palestinian population.[33] Arabs on the whole believe that Israel destroyed villages in order to prevent the return of the refugees. Walid Khalidi conducted field research in which he reports that the Israeli military forces destroyed and depopulated over 400 Palestinian villages in 1948.[34]

On the whole, Arab masses look at Palestine from the Mediterranean to the River Jordan as being part of the Arab and Islamic land that belongs exclusively to the Palestinians. To them, Israel was planted by Great Britain. The Israelis, according to this narrative, are nothing but a bunch of settlers that do not belong to the land of Palestine but sought to empty it of its indigenous Palestinian population and replace them.[35] Seen in this way, the establishment of the state of Israel was rejected from the start but also caused a perception of victimization on the part of the Arabs, particularly the Palestinian refugees. These events and others (see below) have shaped the public attitude towards Israel. They perceive Israel as an expansionist state that should be checked and their understanding of the history of Israeli–Arab interaction is a function of this perspective. Of course, the hegemonic discourses mentioned in the previous chapters have contributed to this perspective.

From the establishment of Israel until 1956, Israel and the Arabs thought a second round of war was approaching. What beefed up this impression was the continuing Arab infiltration into what became Israel accompanied by Israeli retaliatory policies that led to the killing of many Palestinians, Jordanians, Syrians, and Egyptians. After the displacement and dispossession of some 750,000 Palestinians from their towns and houses in what became Israel in 1948, many of them (who were civilians) crossed the armistice lines back into Israel after the fighting had ended. The reasons for their infiltration were, as Benny Morris clarifies in his book, mainly socio-economic rather than political and military.[36] After research in Israeli archives, Benny Morris categorizes the motives behind Palestinian refugee infiltration. The reasons range from their desire to return to their homes, to harvest their fields, to recover their material belongings and sometimes to exact revenge. Some of the infiltrators were nomadic Bedouins who did not understand the meaning of international borders, and some infiltrations were motivated by military and political reasons. Yet according to the best available sources, some 90% of the infiltration between 1949–56 was for social and economic reasons.[37]

Israel saw infiltration as a threat to its day-to-day security.[38] So the Israeli army adopted a hard-hitting policy known as the 'free fire' policy. As the years went on the infiltrators began to respond in kind thus aggravating Israeli fears. But Israeli retaliation became disproportionate. Some 5,000 infiltrators were killed by the Israeli army in the period from 1949–56, the majority of them unarmed.[39] The policy of retaliation aroused the Arabs and instilled in them more hatred towards Israel. It also invited international condemnation. By far the most outrageous Israeli attack took place in 1953 when the reprisal policy took a dreadful turn and Israeli units attacked a Jordanian village called Qibya. The attack was so brutal that it was condemned by the international community. The Israeli government itself was embarrassed by the brutality of the attack and Ben-Gurion decided to issue a statement denying any IDF involvement in the raid.[40]

Another major incident that convinced the Arab masses that Israel was a pawn for forces of imperialism, was when Israel conspired with Britain and France to launch what is known as the Tripartite Aggression (the Suez crisis) against Egypt in 1956. This aggression was seen by the Arab masses as clear proof that Israel was expansionist. Furthermore, a series of Israeli policies only reinforced this image. It will suffice here to point out the Israeli attack on the West Bank village of Samu in 1966, the war in 1967 and the invasion of Lebanon in 1982.

Interestingly, the invasion of Lebanon came after Egypt had signed a peace treaty with Israel in 1979. Many prominent Egyptian figures supported the peace effort as a sign of historical reconciliation between the Arabs and the Jews. However, their ability to defend their pro-peace position was undermined by the Israeli policy of invasion. Obviously, it takes more than the signature of a peace treaty to fundamentally change the public mood. Despite the Israeli–Egyptian peace treaty of 1979, Egyptians remained skeptical as to whether Israel under Likud was genuine in its peace endeavor. Their stand vis-à-vis Israel is a result of many of Israel's policies in the region, particularly towards the Palestinians. Some Israeli policies caused a lot of mistrust and even hatred among the Arabs. Even those who had been outspoken about advocating peace with Israel fell silent in light of what the Arabs saw as Israeli aggression and its lack of willingness to make peace with the Arabs. For example, Tawfik al-Hakim, a very prominent literary figure in Egypt and throughout the Arab world, had advocated peace with Israel. However, he could not defend his pro-peace position after Israel invaded Lebanon in 1982. He published a short play in an Egyptian daily based on a chat that he envisioned having with Begin. He closed his play by saying that he had been fooled in his quest for peace with Israel and Menacham Begin gave a nod of approval.

Enlightened writers and literary men like Anis Mansour embraced peace with Israel as a first step towards historical reconciliation between the Arabs and Israelis. Apparently, they were driven by the dream of having comprehensive and lasting peace in the Middle East with Israel becoming a normal and peaceful state. Those writers could have contributed towards shaping a favorable environment conducive to peace with Israel. Indeed, Anis Mansour not only publicly advocated the idea of historical reconciliation between the Israelis and the Arabs, but also provided Israeli intellectuals with a forum in which to convey their ideas when he allowed them to write in his weekly magazine, *October*. However, Israel's policies, widely perceived by the Arab masses as aggressive, only frustrated them. The quote below came as a result of Anis's frustration with Israeli policies. He kept silent in the first three weeks of the war but then exploded against the inexcusable Israeli aggression against Lebanon in 1982. In his words:

> There is not a single pen in Egypt which has not cursed Israel. There is not a single voice in Egypt that has not disavowed its previous faith in the possibility of total peace with Israel...the essence of peace is a Palestinian state...otherwise there is no peace even if every single Israeli carried an atomic bomb, and even if American space ships carried every Palestinian to the moon...we had reconciled with Israel, looking forward to a compressive peace...it turned out to be a mistake.[41]

Unsurprisingly, the two peace treaties signed by Israel with both Egypt and Jordan have not yet mitigated the level of popular animosity. For the Arab masses, the core problem with Israel is Palestine and the right of Palestinians to self-determination. Nothing but a comprehensive solution of this problem will lead to a change of the people's hearts. Anis Mansour's experience is replicated by some Jordanian writers, at least in part. Immediately after the signing of the

Oslo Accords in September 1993, some Jordanian writers believed that Israel had opted for peace and they became outspoken regarding the need to deal with Israel in a different yet positive way.

However, the impasse in the peace process and what was seen as Israel's intransigent attitude reversed the early optimistic sentiments from many writers. It will suffice here to mention that in 1994, a majority, 80.2%, of Jordanians supported the King's policies of peace with Israel and the Washington Declaration which formally ended the state of war between the two countries.[42] Yet, Benjamin Netanyahu's ascendance to power in Israel was seen in Jordan as a bad sign of what might come. His policies contributed to Jordanian mistrust of him and his government. For instance in 1997, he ordered a failed operation to assassinate a Jordanian in Amman by poison. This reckless move enraged the King of Jordan who threatened to abrogate the peace treaty unless Israel supplied the antidote.[43] This caused a change in the Jordanian public's image of Israel. According to a 1997 opinion poll, some 81% of a national sample viewed Israel as an enemy, while in the Palestinian refugee camps this opinion was held by some 87%.[44]

If anything, Israel's own policies have undermined those who sought peace with Israel. There is barely an Arab who could identify with Israel's policies of occupation and expansion. Arab authors do not live in a vacuum, on the contrary, they are deeply impacted by Israel's actions. Thus, the continuation of the conflict and the Arabs' perception of Israel's aggression have hindered them from embarking on a process of critical reflection on Israel and the actions to be taken. Seen from this perspective, I make the case that it has been difficult for Arab scholars to treat Israel in pure academic terms. A more dispassionate scholarship has yet to emerge and awaits a solution to the conflict. This is not to justify the underdevelopment of Arab scholarship as much as to explain the difficulties involved.

Conclusions

This chapter has revealed that despite the differences among Arab regimes, they all employed anti-Israeli rhetoric to garner support at home and to disgrace and to discredit other Arab rivals. This was caused by the legitimacy deficit and the discrepancies between the imperatives of state nationalism and pan-Arab unity. The centrality of the Palestinian cause provided the Arab regimes with ammunition for furthering their own political legitimacy. The idea of liberating Palestine from the Zionists remained the declared objective of, and a main pillar in, several regimes during the first two decades of the conflict. On this point, different regimes held the same view. Defection from this stand was not tolerated, as could be seen with the Tunisian President Habib Bourguiba.[45]

The chapter has made the case that the intensive exploitation of the conflict was, in part, meant to strengthen the state vis-à-vis its citizens. The high level of expenditure on security and the army was justified by the need to stand up to external plots and Israel, though in reality, the investment in security was meant to face down potential domestic challenges. Furthermore, the conflict with Israel was used to justify the lack of democracy. The argument was that democracy would allow external penetration of a society that was theoretically at war with Israel. Therefore, the regimes developed a discourse that necessarily over-exaggerated the threat posed by Israel. For this reason, Israel was described in many negative terms.

Obviously, Israel was used by the Arab regimes to silence any domestic opposition and to justify censorship. The resultant discourse was so hegemonic that writers, scholars and pundits could not break with this discourse. The natural outcome of this dynamic was that writing on Israel during the first two decades at least, following the 1948 war, was a failure on a grand scale.

Israel proved to be a handy way of mobilizing the masses behind their despotic leaders. Almost every Arab leader sought to exploit the conflict in one way or another to enhance their domestic as well as regional status. A key argument in this chapter is the exploitation of the conflict and the demonization of Israel as a means to stifle internal problems and bring about political repression that impacted on academic freedom. Put simply, writing on Israel suffered because Israel was used by the regimes for their own legitimacy and regional ambitions. For an extended period of time scholars have substituted ideology for sound critical writing. Israel's policies were seen by the Arab masses as a clear evidence of expansion and arrogance. Therefore, the level of enmity towards Israel should be seen against this background. Writers and authors were influenced by the general public atmosphere defined by animosity to Israel. Holding on to occupied Arab and Palestinian land only furthers the stereotypical image of Israel.

Notes

—–—

1 Mahmoud Darwish was the Palestinian national poet. He was born in Haifa and grew up in what later became Israel. In early 1970 he decided to leave and voluntarily chose to be a refugee. He was seen as the Palestinian resistance poet.

2 Numerous books and articles have been published addressing the Arab order and the fragmentation accompanying this order. Suffice it here to point out to the seminal work of Malcolm Kerr, *The Arab Cold War.*

3 There are two official narratives on the reason behind the influx of Palestinian refugees in 1947/8. Whereas the Arabs blame it on Israel, the latter refused to bear any moral responsibilities for the refugees and maintained that they left on their own. However, the Israeli New Historians seem to vindicate the Arab position. On this see, Benny Morris, *The Birth of the Refugee Problem, 1947–49.*

4 For the then balance of forces between Israel and the Arabs see Avi Shlaim and Eugen Rogan, *The War for Palestine: Rewriting the History of 1948* (Cambridge: Cambridge University Press, 2001).

5 Sati al-Husri, *al-Uruba Awalan* (Arabism First) (Beirut: Dar al-'ilm li al-Malayeen, 1965), p. 149.

6 Nasser was one of the officers who fought the Israelis and his unit was besieged in Faluja. That experience impacted deeply his thinking on Israel.

7 For his belief system see Mohammed al-Sayid Saleem, *Al-Tahlil 'Siyasi 'Nasiri* (Nasserite Political Analysis), p. 147.

8 Adeed Dawisha, *Arab Nationalism in the Twentieth Century: From Triumph to Despair* (Princeton and Oxford: Princeton University press, 2003), p. 142.

9 Malcolm Kerr, *The Arab Cold War.*

10 Michael C. Hudson, *Arab Politics: The Search for Legitimacy* (New Haven and London: Yale University Press, 1977), p. 2.

11   Michael C. Hudson, *The Search for Legitimacy*, p. 3.

12   Avraham Sela, *The Decline of the Arab-Israeli Conflict: Middle East Politics and the Quest for Regional Order* (New York: State University of New York Press, 1998), p. 27.

13   www.freedomhouse.org, accessed September 2007.

14   Bernard Lewis, *The Middle East and the West* (New York: Harper Torchbooks, 1964), p. 48.

15   Lisa Anderson, "Democracy in the Arab World: A Critique of the Political Cultural Approach", in Rex Brynen, Bahgat Korany and Paul Noble (eds.), *Political Liberalization and Democratization in the Arab World* (Boulder: Lynne Rienner Publishers, 1995), pp. 77–92.

16   Nazih Ayubi, *Overstating the Arab State: Politics and Society in the Middle East* (London: Tauris, 1995). The term 'Asiatic mode of production' is a concept in the theory of historical materialism that describes a widespread pre-Capitalist mode of production, in which irrigation agriculture plays an important role in organizing power relations in society. This mode of production led to the rise of Oriental despotism. The term was probably coined by Karl Marx, and reflects widely-held views of the world at that time.

17   Giacomo Luciani and Hazem Beblawi (eds.), *The Rentier State* (London: Croom Helm, 1987).

18   For an interesting discussion on this point, see Brent E. Sasley, "The Role of the Arab-Israeli Conflict in Arab Domestic Policy: Using International Relations for Internal Consumption", a paper prepared for the 43rd Annual Convention of the International Studies Association, New Orleans, Louisiana, 24–27 March, 2002.

19   *The Arab Human Development Report* (New York, NY: United Nations Development Programme, Regional Bureau for Arab States, 2002).

20   Asher Susser, *On Both Banks of the Jordan: A Political Biography of Wasfi Al-Tall* (London: Frank Cass, 1994).

21   Discussion with Ghazi Sa'di at the Jalil Center, Amman, 22 October 2002.

22   For an interesting analysis on this point, see Avraham Sela, "Arab Historiography of the 1948 War: The Quest for Legitimacy", in

Laurence J. Silberstein (ed.), *New Perspectives on Israeli History: The Early Years of the State* (New York and London: New York University Press, 1991), p. 125.

23 Benny Morris discusses in detail how they were ordered to leave by the Israeli forces. In his account, Ben-Gurion himself gave orders to his general to force the Palestinians out of these two towns. For more details, see Benny Morris, *The Birth of the Palestinian Refugee Problem.*

24 King Abullah Ibn al-Hussein, *My Memoirs Completed "Al-Takmila"* (London; New York: Longman, 1978).

25 Mahmud al-Russan, *Ma'arik Bab al-Wad* (The Battles of Bab al-Wad) (Amman: n.d [1950?]).

26 Abdullah al-Tell, *Karitht Filastine, Mudhakarat Abdullah al-Tell, Qa'id Ma'rakat al-Quds* (The Catastrophe of Palestine, Memoirs of Abdullah al-Tell, the Leader of Jerusalem Battle) (Cairo: Dar Al-Huda, 1959).

27 Suleiman al-Musa, *Ayam la Tunsa, al-Urdun fi Harab 1948* (Days That Cannot be Forgotten, Jordan in the 1948 War) (Amman: 1982).

28 For a good revision of Arab historiography on the war, see Avraham Sela, "Arab Historiography of the 1948 War: The Quest for Legitimacy", pp. 124–54.

29 Fouad Ajami, "The End of Pan-Arabism", *Foreign Affairs*, vol. 57, no. 2 (Winter 1978/79), p. 356.

30 Discussion with Ahmed Khalifa, a senior researcher at the Institute for Palestinian Studies, Amman, 22 October 2002.

31 Arab media and press are usually full of articles, reports and commentaries echoing these themes.

32 In a recent book, a former Israeli Minister of Foreign Affairs discusses the concept of transfer in Zionist thinking. For more details see Shlomo Ben-Ami, *Scars of War, Wounds of Peace: The Israeli–Arab Tragedy* (Oxford and New York: Oxford University Press, 2006), chapter two.

33 This massacre was perpetrated by *Irgun* and *Lehi* with the *Haganah's* collusion. It took place on 9 April 1948 when joint forces of the right wing *Irgun* and *Lehi* attacked the village of Deir Yassin killing some

250 Palestinians and forcing the rest to flee. It is widely believed that this massacre caused panic among Palestinians and many were intimidated by how far the Zionists were prepared to go. Israeli New Historian Benny Morris confirmed that this massacre took place and argues that the *Haganah* (the Israeli official army) consented to the massacre.

34 For the demolition of over than 400 Arab villages, see Walid Khalidi (ed.), *All That Remains: The Palestinian Villages Occupied and Depopulated by Israel in 1948* (Washington, DC: Institute for Palestinian Studies, 1992).

35 Mustafa Elwi, "Al-Bu'd Al-'Strateji Lisra' Al-'Rabi Al-Israeli" (The Strategic Dimension of the Arab–Israeli Conflict), in Hassan Naeh (ed.), *Intifadat al aqsa wa garn men 'sria'* (Al-Aqsa Intifada and a Century of Conflict) (Amman: Mu'sasat Abdel-hamid Shoman, 2002), pp. 161–3.

36 Benny Morris, *Israel's Border Wars, 1949–1956: Arab Infiltration, Israeli Retaliation and the Countdown to the Suez War* (Oxford: Clarendon Press, 1993).

37 Benny Morris, *ibid.*, p. 49.

38 The Israeli governments did not view the infiltration activities as a threat to its basic security (the existence of the state) but rather to the lives of Israeli individuals.

39 Benny Morris, *Israel's Border Wars, 1949–1956: Arab Infiltration, Israeli Retaliation and the Countdown to the Suez War*, p. 412.

40 On the night of 14–15 October 1953, Israeli Unit 101, led by Ariel Sharon, attacked Qibya following the murder of an Israeli woman and her two children by infiltrators. The Israeli unit penetrated into Qibya, blew up houses, and inflicted a heavy death toll on the population. After the attack the Qibya village was reduced to a pile of debris. Sixty-nine civilians, the majority of them women and children, were killed.

41 Anis Mansour, *Al-Ahram*, 17 July 1982.

42 More details of the opinion poll are available at the Center for Strategic Studies at the University of Jordan, www.css-jordan.org (Accessed 15 October 2006).

43 Hassan A. Barari, *Jordan and Israel: Ten Years Later* (Amman: CSS, 2004).

44 More details of the opinion poll are available at the Center for Strategic Studies at the University of Jordan, www.css-jordan.org (Accessed 20 December 2006).

45 In 1965, Tunisian President Bourguiba suggested that the Arabs should consider negotiating with Israel and recognize it within the boundaries of the Partition Plan of 1947. His statements took everyone by surprise. All Arab leaders roundly rebuked him, and some even went as far as accusing him of being part of a conspiracy against Arab rights in Palestine. Accordingly, he was ostracized in inter-Arab politics for years.

5

Conclusions and the Current Scene

——

If anything, this book has demonstrated how many of scholarly works have been marred by the inability, or worse the unwillingness, of writers and authors to go beyond the hegemonic and ideological discourses. Israelism is the resultant mode of writing and scholarship, writing which has, to a great extent, suffered from an inherent bias in Arab scholars' study of Israel. Much of their understanding of Israel and the Arab–Israeli conflict has been rigidly tied to a framework that is highly informed by two components: the hegemonic discourse and the conflict prism. The outcome, as discussed throughout this book, has been the underdevelopment of Israeli studies in the Meshreq Arab countries.

Apparently, it is hard for Arab scholars to write on Israel with any kind of detachment, in the end, they all have their own political stands. It goes without saying that intellectuals, on the whole, feel some kind of ethical and political duty that pervades their writing on a specific topic. This leads to unconscious tension between the imperative of sound scholarship, which entails some degree of objectivity, and the tremendous impact of ideology, which assumes no standard of objectivity at all.[1] Yet detachment does not mean that you are indifferent. On the contrary, and particularly in the Israeli case, detachment and impartiality could help Arab scholars see things as they are. It would have yielded a far better understanding of Israel that would have helped in the planning process and the decision on whether to engage Israel in peace or war. Herein lies the heart of the matter: Arab authors' submission to the prevalent hegemonic discourse has produced more myths than realities.

Undoubtedly, writing on the conflict with Israel is a highly charged topic both politically and emotionally. Throughout the years of the conflict, an intellectual mainstream has emerged that has both controlled and defined the terms by which Israel should be understood. More troubling still is that it delineates boundaries of a legitimate or illegitimate debate. Take, for instance, the phenomenon of suicide bombing carried out by Hamas against Israelis during the al-Aqsa Intifada. The mainstream opinion among the Arabs was that suicide bombing was one manifestation of martyrdom and resistance and therefore legitimate.[2] For a while, it was unthinkable to write about the use of suicide bombing in terms other than to describe it as a legitimate tool against the Israeli occupation of Palestinian land. Arab writers who wrote against it on moral and political grounds were immediately described as unpatriotic or as belonging to the culture of defeatism. Those who wrote against it were soon punished by other outspoken writers who launched a campaign to silence any intellectual inquiry that criticized the suicide operation.

It is not a secret that the Palestinian cause is the number one issue for all Arabs. Hence, it should not be surprising that most of the coverage of Israel, especially in the media, is on conflict with Israel. It is not difficult to spot that numerous people, regardless of their qualifications and knowledge, write and publish on Israel. Volumes of mistakes are made as many of these writers write to address the emotions of the masses. What propels this kind of 'bad' writing is the fact that it is the most acceptable to the media. This kind of propagandist writing is very emotive and capable of mobilizing the masses and does not clash with the masses' passionate attachment to the Palestinians' cause. Therefore, a great deal of writing on Israel is a mere repetition and re-cycling of what has already been written, lacks sophisticated analysis and provides no contribution worth speaking of.

This book has set out the political, intellectual and historical contexts that have helped create such a mindset. While taking into account the unique historical context, the book has also analyzed the scholarly work pertaining to how Israel has been written about. It has examined the authors' bias and belief system and explored how a hegemonic discourse has delineated the process of interpretation of Israel. It has also showed that this inherent bias is caused by the predominance of two assumptions that have informed the ontology and epistemology of Israeli studies in the Meshreq. The first one maintains that Israel is nothing but an artificial entity that was planted by imperial powers and has no independence of its own. The second belief stems from a political and ideological conviction that Israel is not here to stay. This has created a sort of inevitability syndrome – the belief that Israel will vanish as the crusaders did centuries ago.

On the whole, the most prominent trend in studying Israel remains an ideological one that suffers significantly from a deficit in epistemologies, which has hindered the development of genuine and sincere study of Israel in the Arab world. Academic scholarship remains a prisoner to ideology and the doggedness of the conflict with Israel. The hegemony of these ideological trends has given scholars and writers little room to maneuver. As a consequence, most writers have been plagued by a closed belief system that tends to cast off any new information that does not conform to their beliefs. Therefore, they have inadvertently subordinated critical writing and sound scholarship to the imperatives of settling an account with the enemy.

As mentioned in my introduction, the current scene is not entirely gloomy. Among the hundreds of titles written there are some good books and papers. Notwithstanding the picture painted by the above analysis, the situation has improved slightly in several respects in the last decades, though not sufficiently. Some good scholars have made names for themselves: Emad Gad, Azmi Bishara, Adel Manna and Majid Al-Hajj are good scholars who write on Israel with a reasonable degree of objectivity while maintaining their fundamental political stands vis-à-vis the conflict with Israel. Some Arab research centers have also launched programs for the systematic study of Israeli society and politics. Al-Ahram Center for Political and Strategic Studies has published a monthly bulletin called *Mukhtarat Israeliya* for over a decade, in which many articles from the Hebrew press are translated well. In addition, the center has published a series of books that can be seen as examples of good scholarship. In Ramallah, the Palestinians established *Madar*: the Palestinian Forum for Israeli Studies. This forum was established in 2000 with the purpose of presenting the political, social and economic scenes in Israel to a wider Arab audience. What distinguishes this center is its reliance on good scholars from among Israeli Arabs. These scholars have the advantage of having lived in Israel for all of their lives, and have graduated from Israeli universities and know Hebrew very well. *Madar* publishes a regular journal in Arabic called *Israeli Issues*. From my reading of some issues, I can categorize this product as good, though it could be further improved. The current scene and the slight improvement in the status of the Israeli studies does not mean that the problem articulated throughout this book has disappeared, but I do not want the qualitative improvement of some studies to go wholly unnoticed.

With few exceptions, the current scene focuses mainly on issues relevant to Israel's foreign policy. Yet, while one can discern improvement in the state of the literature on Israel, still one can safely make the case that it suffers from polarization. Clearly the polarization is linked to an age-old problem in studying international relations known as the level of analysis problem.[3] In other words, what level of analysis should we focus on to account for a certain outcome? Should we be looking at the unit (the state), the system, or the leaders? In his excellent exposition of how Israeli society works amid the persistence of the second Intifada, Azmi Bishara points to the problem of analysis in current Arab writing on Israel.[4] He criticizes a new emerging trend in writing that views Israeli domestic politics as the key political factor in the region. Bishara rightly argues that this trend misuses the call to study Israeli society. According to Bishara, this trend tends to make a mountain out of a molehill when, for instance, a personal rivalry surfaces between two Israeli leaders. The second trend views the social and political strife within Israel as nothing but a conspiracy and a division of roles among Israeli politicians. For those who adopt this view, the real social, political, economic and cultural struggle within Israel is at best an act.

While I concur with Bishara in his observation, the fact remains that there are some Arab writers and scholars, as mentioned above, who manage to study Israel by applying the universally accepted tools of analysis in social disciplines. These scholars keep their political anti-occupation stands but manage to write on Israel with a degree of detachment and objectivity. Azmi Bishara is an epitome of the scholars who write with a profound knowledge on Israel without compromising their political and ideological preferences. This trend should be encouraged. Khalil Shikaki and Abdel Monem Said can be seen in this light as well. That said, and despite occasional landmarks, the study of Israel in the Arab Meshreq has failed to produce systemic and groundbreaking results.

This book does not aim only at offering a critique of the status of Israeli studies in the Arab world. In fact one of my motives in writing this critique is to draw attention to the problem and to stir a debate on how to develop Israeli studies in the Arab world. There are some objective conditions that impede the development of Israeli studies which we can do little as scholars to change. An example of these conditions is lack of academic and political freedom, a wider societal problem which scholars cannot do much about. But there are some other conditions which we can certainly create to improve the situation, such as pursuing high standards of scholarship and objectivity in the classroom and research. To achieve these ends we need to fulfill two preconditions: we must have a corps of well-qualified scholars and we must establish disciplinary standards. I believe that the first condition can be accomplished due to my belief in the presence of excellent scholars in the Arab world, Arabs who are limited only by the obstacles that the book has outlined. Therefore, creating an epistemic community to discuss how to develop this field is a must if we aspire to the pooling of resources in order to create a better degree of scholarship. As for disciplinary standards, we do not have to invent them because they already exist, but we do need to internalize the need to adopt them and stop thinking that the issue of Israel is exceptional and cannot be studied by the existing disciplinary methods.

Further, we are badly in need of a corps of scholars who know Hebrew and who are willing to spend lengthy periods of time in Israel. It will be useful if a younger generation of scholars internalize the benefit of learning Hebrew and of spending time in Israel. Their knowledge will be enhanced enormously. I am aware that it is not easy for scholars to visit and stay in Israel. The problem is related to a wider issue, i.e., normalization. Many intellectuals in Egypt and Jordan were blacklisted and on some occasions kicked out of their associations for daring to visit Israel. Unsurprisingly, few are willing to pay the high price for taking such a stand. Those who have spearheaded the campaign to delegitimize dealings with the Israelis have failed to show how a boycott benefits the Arab or the Palestinian cause. How have we hurt Israel by ignoring it?

The opposite is true. The existence of a great number of 'experts' who lack the necessary academic competence or are not qualified on the basis of their language competence or length of residence in Israel has hurt the Arab side more than it has benefited them. Yet, the Arabs will do themselves a big favor if they can tolerate students and scholars traveling to and staying in Israel. It is only then that they will be able to learn Hebrew properly and understand how Israeli society functions. Without doing this, Arab scholars run the risk of perpetuating modest, albeit slightly improving, Israeli studies.

In a nutshell, Arab writings on Israel intertwined politics and scholarship to present a politically and emotionally charged topic. While the influence of religion and pan-Arabism and its discourse greatly affected the mass perception of Israel, the driving force behind the masses' hatred for Israel, and the scholar's bias in writing about Israel, has more to do with the political reality, and the need for the continuation of the conflict, than it does with ideological beliefs. Simply put, the continuation of the Arab–Israeli conflict has further fueled the Arabs' sense of frustration and victimization and provided them with a prism that includes the already mentioned ideological dimensions. For this reason, the belief that Israel will vanish, and the belief that the West has been the life force behind the establishment and continuing existence of Israel, have relegated studying Israel from within especially during the first two decades of the conflict. The fact that Israel is now an independent force capable of functioning and surviving on its own, independent of Western support, has been missed by Arab writers for an extended period of time.

Notes

——

1   Bernard Barber, *Intellectual Pursuits: Toward an Understanding of Culture* (New York: Rowman and Littlefield, 1998), pp. 109–38.

2   For more details on this see, Hassan Barari, "Ta'theer al-'Intifada 'la Al-Ra'I al-'am fi Israel" ("The Impact of the Intifada on Public Opinion in Israel"), in Emad Gad (ed.), *Intifadat al-Aqsa: Tumuh al-Fikra was Azmat al'Idarah* (Al-Aqsa Intifada: the Ambition of the Idea and the Crisis in Management (Cairo: Al-Ahram Center for Strategic and Political Studies, 2002), pp. 131–62.

3   For more details of this theoretical dilemma, see David Singer, "The Level of Analysis Problem in International Relations", in Knorr Klaus and Verba Sidney (eds.), *The International System: Theoretical Essays* (Princeton, NJ: Princeton University Press, 1961), pp. 77–92.

4   Azmi Bishara, *Al-Intifada wal Mujtama' Al-Israeli: Tahlil fi Khidam al-Ahdath* (The Intifada and Israeli Society: Analysis Amid Events), p. 117.

Epilogue

— —

After I finished writing this book, I took a step back and started to think about what was missing. There is no claim whatsoever made that this book presents the most perfect perspective of the topic under study. It is meant first and foremost to be a catalyst for a healthy and constructive debate on the issue.

One might well also ask about the flip side. Is it not unfair to claim that Arab scholars alone have been prejudiced in their study of the other? What about the other side? Do we not also need to examine how Arab studies have been developed in Israel? Undoubtedly, studying how Israeli scholars have studied Arab societies and politics is an equally important step if we are to have a better appreciation of the deep-seated mutual animosity. Tempting as it may be, this job falls beyond the scope of my inquiry. However,

I will briefly state my assumption about that topic, and my impression of its effect.

My assumption is that there is a strong link between nation building and the collective memory of a people. This impression, which is based on my reading of Hebrew, is that Israeli governments, particularly in the formative years of the educational system, deliberately imparted to the people an official national narrative which depicted the conflict in a particular way. It was a critical step, from the Zionist perspective, to make sure that all internal differences were kept at bay, given the 'imminent' threat posed by the Arabs, who had been outraged to politicide. Israel was presented as a tiny 'David' which fought heroically against an Arab 'Goliath'. The Arabs alone, according to this mode of thinking, were to blame for the catastrophe that befell the Palestinians in 1948.

Obviously, this Israeli narrative has not been helpful for historical reconciliation. Explicit in this kind of rhetoric is that Israel would outright reject any peace deal involving the return of refugees. Indeed, this narrative is meant to forge a kind of collective national memory but in the process has created more myths than realities. While writing history is a very important process, the Israeli historians were driven partly by the need to win in terms of narratives. Put simply, it is a war over narrative at a time when Israelis and Arabs contest the same piece of land. Unsurprisingly, the Arab–Israeli conflict remains the lens through which many Israeli scholars interpret Arab societies and politics.

Like Arab regimes who have sought to portray a certain image of Israel, Israeli governments have controlled education, and the Ministry of Education has determined what has been included and excluded in the school curricula.

While this helps Israel, the government has also run the risk of manipulating the collective memory of Israelis. The state manipulated the past to mold Israelis' perceptions for years to come. The outcome is that Arabs are stereotyped in the minds of many Israelis. There has been a process to delegitimize Arab claims to the land and to dehumanize Arabs to justify harsh policies against Palestinians.

This mindset produced many books, most importantly text books (especially during the first few decades of the conflict) which were brimming with misconceptions and stereotypes that resulted in a kind of institutionalization of the negative attitudes towards Arabs in general. Terms such as "terrorists", "sly", "cheat", "thief", and "robber" were typical adjectives used in these books in reference to Arabs. Anita Shapira, a well-known Israeli historian, pointed out this fact in her famous book *Land and Power* and argues that the mutual violent and deep antipathy between the two sides of the conflict has created a tendency to dehumanize Arabs as a way to justify the use of violence against them.[1]

The curricula in religious schools (*yishivot*) presents the land as eternally belonging to the Jews exclusively. Mercaz Ha-Rav is a prominent school (*yeshiva*) which turned out many students who forged the *Gush Emunim* movement (an extra-parliamentarian movement), which in turn spearheaded the settlement movement. Needless to say, the existence of settlements has contributed significantly to the failure of the peace process. Under the mentorship of Rabbi Zvi Yehuda Kook, the school instilled in the minds of students the need to redeem the Palestinian territories by physically settling there. For this movement, establishing settlements was a divine duty that could accelerate the advent of the Messiah.

Evidently, by manipulating the narrative, the Israeli government created perceptions amongst Israelis which did not help the peace process. People tend to react to perceptions rather than reality. The problem with perceptions in this case is that they are articulated in ethnocentric terms. Ethnocentric opinions often lead to exclusive narratives which negate the foe's narratives. These dichotomous ethnocentric narratives are often accompanied, according to Ellie Podeh from Indiana University, by misconception, stereotypes, and prejudice. They are a key tool in the process of dehumanization.[2]

Ethnocentrism is aggravated in the case of Israel with the existence of *yishvot*, Israeli religious schools which give a kind of absolutism to the way Arabs are portrayed. The Mercaz Ha-Rav in Jerusalem is a typical example of a school that produced generations of settlers who believed that the land was theirs and that the Arabs were usurpers. When we put this idea in juxtaposition with the same notion adopted by Islamists, one can understand why historical reconciliation is such an uphill battle.

Until recently, the Israeli educational system has been dominated by the national Zionist narrative of history, with a predictably Zionist spin on the messages conveyed. However, with the advent of "New History", another dynamic came into play. The official Zionist narrative is no longer the only one in Israel. Since the late 1980s, it has been challenged by the rise of a group of Israeli historians who were quickly dubbed "New Historians" and who offered a revisionist history of what happened before, during, and after the 1948 war. Avi Shlaim, Benny Morris, Ilan Pappé, and Simha Flapan, to name but a few, used the declassified Israeli archives and came up with a different narrative. They debunked the myths that had been propagated in the official narrative regarding the war and the refugees.

The most thought-provoking theme is the one presented by Benny Morris in his books on the refugee problem. His writing was perhaps the most eye-opening, focusing on Israel's contribution to the Palestinian *nakba* (catastrophe). While he denies the Arab claim that there was a political plan to expel the Palestinians, he conceded that thousands of them *were* expelled, as was the case in Lydda and Ramleh, two cities that Israel occupied in 1948, by a direct order from the Israeli leadership. Many argue that Morris's exposition of the refugee problem amounts to his grudging acknowledgement that Israel had an interest in bringing about what is known in today's language as ethnic cleansing.

Paradoxically, Benny Morris' thorough analysis of the situation has not caused him to adopt a peaceful approach to the conflict. He is angry at the Palestinians because of the eruption of the second Intifada. Therefore, in an interview he gave to the *Haaretz* newspaper, he said that Israel had made a mistake in not expelling *all* the Palestinians in 1948. In his words: "Ben-Gurion was right. If he had not done what he did, a state would not have come into being. That has to be clear. It is impossible to evade it. Without the uprooting of the Palestinians, a Jewish state would not have arisen here."[3] While this is a political right-wing stand, Morris' subsequent works are still written with objective, academic detachment.

To sum up, although the work of the new historians has come a long way and has made major inroads into debunking the myths of the conflict, a study on how Israeli scholars have studied the Arab world is in order. A more objective way of presenting the Arabs might be a step in the right direction in the long path toward historical reconciliation between Israelis and the Arabs. As they say, 'it takes two to tango'; both parties in the conflict need to internalize the importance of this step in peacemaking.

Notes

1 Anita Shapira, *Land and Power: The Zionist Resort to Force, 1881–1948* (New York: Oxford University Press, 1992), p. 362.
2 Ellie Podeh, "History and Memory in the Israeli Educational System: The Portrayal of the Arab–Israeli Conflict in History Textbooks (1948–2000)", *History & Memory* 12.1 (2000), pp. 65–100.
3 Ari Shavit, "Survival of the Fittest", *Haaretz*, 8 January 2004.

Bibliography

Adwan, Sami and Dan Bar-On, "Learning Each Other's Historical Narratives: In Israeli and Palestinians Schools", http://www.vispo.com/PRIME/leohn.htm (Accessed 20 June 2007).

Ajami, Fouad, "The End of Pan-Arabism", *Foreign Affairs*, vol. 57, no. 2 (Winter 1978/79), pp. 355–73.

Ali, Mohammed Ali and Ibrahim al-Himssani, *Israel Qa'eda 'Dwaniya* (Israel: An Aggressive Base) (Cairo: Addar Al-Qawmiyya Litiba'ah Wanahir).

Ali, Mohammed Ali, *Fi Dakhil Israel: Dirasat Kiyanaha Al-Siyasi Wal 'Iqtisadi* (Inside Israel: A study on its Political and Economic Entity) (Cairo).

Anderson, Lisa, "Democracy in the Arab World: A Critique of the Political Cultural Approach", in Rex Brynen, Bahgat Korany and Paul Noble (eds.),

Political Liberalization and Democratization in the Arab World (Boulder: Lynne Rienner Publishers, 1995), pp. 77–92.

Al-Astal, Kamal Mohammed, *Mustaqbal Israel Bayn Al-'Sti'sal wat Tadweeb* (The Future of Israel Between Elimination and Assimilation) (Cairo: Dar 'Lmawqif Al-'Arabi, 1980).

Ataya, Mahmoud Amin, *Al-Nizam Sharq Awsati Al-Jadid: Al-Mukhatatat Al-Israeliya Lilhaymanah Ala Elmantiqa Al-Arabiya* (Middle Eastern Order: Israeli Schemes for Hegemony Over the Arab Area) (Beirut: Al-Manara, 1995).

Ayubi, Nazih N., *Overstating the Arab State: Politics and Society in the Middle East* (London: Tauris, 1995).

Azzam, Maha, "Islamism Revisited", *International Affairs*, vol. 82, no. 6 (2006), pp. 1119–32.

Al-Banna, Hassan, *Mudhakarat Al-Da'wa Wi Da'iya* (Memories of the Call and the Caller) (Cairo: Dar El-Shihab), pp. 228–30.

Barari, Hassan A., *Israeli Politics and the Middle East Peace Process, 1988–2002* (London and New York: Routledge, 2004).

Barari, Hassan A., *Jordan and Israel: Ten Years Later* (Amman: CSS, 2004).

Barari, Hassan A., "Ta'theer al-'Intifada 'la Al-Ra'I al-'am fi Israel" (The Impact of the Intifada on Public Opinion in Israel), in Emad Gad (ed.), *Intifadat al-Aqsa: Tumuh al-Fikra was Azmat al'Idarah* (Al-Aqsa Intifada: the Ambition of the Idea and the Crisis in Management (Cairo: Al-Ahram Center for Strategic and Political Studies, 2002), pp. 131–62.

Barber, Bernard, *Intellectual Pursuits: Toward an Understanding of Culture* (New York: Rowman and Littlefield, 1998), pp. 109–38.

Barnett, Michael N., *Dialogues in Arab Politics: Negotiations in Regional Order* (New York: Columbia University Press, 1998).

Beinin, Joel, *Was the Red Flag Flying There? Marxist Politics and the Arab–Israeli Conflict in Egypt and Israel, 1948–1965* (Berkeley and Los Angeles: University of California Press, 1990).

Ben-Ami, Shlomo, *Scars of War, Wounds of Peace: The Israeli–Arab Tragedy* (Oxford and New York: Oxford University Press, 2006).

Binder, Leonard, *The Study of the Middle East: Research and Scholarship in the Humanities and the Social Sciences* (New York and London: John Wiley & Sons, 1976).

Bishara, Azmi, *Al-Intifada wal Mujtama' Al-Israeli: Tahlil fi Khidam al-Ahdath* (The Intifada and Israeli Society: Analysis Amid Events) (Beirut: Markiz Dirasat Al-Wahda Al-Arabiya, 2002).

Booth, Ken, *Strategy and Ethnocentrism* (London: Croom Helm, 1979).

Brown, Nathan, Amr Hamzawy, and Marina Ottaway, "Islamist Movements and the Democratic Process in the Arab World: Exploring Gray Zones", *Carnegie Paper*, no. 67 (March 2006).

Dawisha, Adeed, *Arab Nationalism in the Twentieth Century: From Triumph to Despair* (Princeton and Oxford: Princeton University Press, 2003).

Elmessiri, Abdelwahab, *Al-Suhyunia wal 'Unf: Min Bidayat Al-Istitan Ila Intifadat Al-Aqsa* (Zionism and Violence:

From the Beginning of Settlement to the Al-Aqsa Initfada) (Cairo: Dar-Elshuruq, 2001).

Elmessiri, Abdelwahab, *Al-Suhyuniya wa Naziya wa Nihayat Al-Tarikh* (Zionism, Nazism, and End of History) (Cairo: Dar-Elshuruq, 2001).

Elmessiri, Abdelwahab, *Inhiyar Israel Min 'Dakhil* (Collapse of Israel from Within) (Cairo: Dar 'lma'arif, 2001).

Elmessiri, Abdelwahab, *Mauso'at al-Yahud, al-Yahudiya wal Suhyuniya: Namozaj Tafsiri* (Encyclopedia of the Jews, Judaism, and Zionism: A New Explanatory Paradigm (Cairo: Dar-Elshuruq, 1999, 8 volumes).

Elmessiri, Abdelwahab, Interview, www.arabiyat.com (Last Accessed 2 November 2006).

Elwi, Mustafa, "Al-Bu'd Al-'Strateji Lisra' Al-'Rabi Al-Israeli" (The Strategic Dimension of the Arab–Israeli Conflict), in Hassan Naeh (ed.), *Intifadat al aqsa wa garn men 'sria'* (Al-Aqsa Intifada and a Century of Conflict) (Amman: Mu'sasat Abdel-Hamid Shoman, 2002), pp. 161–75.

Fanon, Frantz, *A Dying Colonialism* (New York: Grove Press, 1965), translated from French.

Fanon, Frantz, *The Wretched of the Earth* (New York: Grove Press, 1963), translated from French.

Faraj, Ali Miss'ad Taha, *Israel, 'La 'Ayn?!: Dirasah Fi Fikr Wa Tarikh Al-Yahud Wa Massir Dawlatuhum 'Lhaliya* (Israel, Where to?!: A Study in the Thinking and History of the Jews and the Destiny of their Current State) (Cairo: Ein For Human and Social Studies, 1999).

Faraj, Mohammed Abd al-Salam, "The Absent Duty", in Rifaat Sayed Ahmed (ed.), *The Militant Prophet: The Revolutionaries*, vol. 2 (London: Riad El-Rayyes Books, 1991), pp. 137–49.

Gad, Emad (ed.), *Al-Intikhabat Al-Israeliya 2003: Al-Amn Awalan* (Israeli Election 2003: Security First) (Cairo: Al-Ahram Center for Strategic and Political Studies, 2003).

Gerges, Fawaz A., *The Far Enemy: Why Jihad Went Global* (New York: Cambridge University Press, 2005).

Hudson, Michael C., *Arab Politics: The Search for Legitimacy* (New Haven and London: Yale University Press, 1977).

Al-Husri, Sati, *al-'Uruba Awalan* (Arabism First) (Beirut: Dar al-'ilm li al-Malayeen, 1965).

Al-Husri, Sati, *Ma Hiya al-Qawmiya: Abhath wa Disrasat 'ala Dhaw'I al-Ahdath wa al-Nadhariyat* (What is Nationalism?: Enquiries and Studies in Light of Events and Theories) (Beirut: Dar al-'ilm li al-Malayeen, 1963).

Ibn al-Hussein, King Abdullah, *My Memoirs Completed "Al-Takmila"* (London; New York: Longman, 1978).

Ibrahim, Saad Eddin, "Domestic Developments in Egypt", in William Quandt (ed.), *The Middle East: Ten Years After Camp David* (Washington, DC: Brookings Institution, 1988), pp. 19–63.

Kautsky, Karl, *Socialism and Colonial Policy: An Analysis* (Belfast: Athol Books, 1975).

Kerr, Malcolm H., *The Arab Cold War: Gamal 'Abd Al-Nasir and His Rivals, 1958–1970* (Oxford and New York: Oxford University Press, 1971).

Khadduri, Walid, "Al-Qawmiya al-'Arabiya wa al-Dimuquatiya: Muraja'a Naqdiya" (Arab Nationalism and Democracy: A Critical Review), *Al-Mustaqbal al-'Arabi*, no. 228 (February 1998).

Khalidi, Walid (ed.), *All That Remains: The Palestinian Villages Occupied and Depopulated by Israel in 1948*

(Washington, DC: Institute for Palestinian Studies, 1992).

Korany, Bahgat, "International Relations Theory: Contributions for Research in the Middle East", in Mark Tessler (ed), *Area Studies and Social Science: Strategies for Understanding Middle East Politics* (Bloomington & Indianapolis: Indiana University Press, 1999), pp. 148–49.

Lawson, Fred H., *Why Syria Goes to War: Thirty Years of Confrontation* (Ithaca and London: Cornell University Press, 1996).

Lenin, V. I., *Imperialism, The Highest Stage of Capitalism: A Popular Outline* (Peking: Foreign Languages Press, 1965), first published 1917.

Lewis, Bernard, *The Middle East and the West* (New York: Harper Torchbooks, 1964).

Luciani, Giacomo and Hazem Beblawi (eds.), *The Rentier State* (London: Croom Helm, 1987).

Maclean, John, "Belief Systems and Ideology in International Relations: A Critical Approach", in Richard Little and Steve Smith (eds.), *Belief System and International Relations* (Oxford: Basil Blackwell Ltd, 1988), pp. 57–82.

Manna, Adel and Azmi Bishara (eds.), *Dirasat fil Mujtama' Al-israeli* (Studies on Israeli Society) (Israel: Center for Arab Society in Israel, 1995) (in Arabic).

Marx, Karl, *Capital* (Chicago, Ill: Encyclopedia Britannica, c. 1952).

Marx, Karl, *The Communist Manifesto* (New York: Washington Square Press, 1964).

Marx, Karl, "The Future Results of British Rule in India", in *The Portable Karl Marx* (New York: Viking Press, 1983).

Marx, Karl and Engels, Frederick, "On Ireland", in *Ireland and the Irish Question; a Collection of Writings* (New York: International Publishers, 1972).

Morris, Benny, *Israel's Border Wars, 1949–1956: Arab Infiltration, Israeli Retaliation, and the Countdown to the Suez War* (Oxford: Clarendon Press, 1993).

Morris, Benny, *The Birth of the Refugee Problem, 1947–49* (Cambridge: Cambridge University Press, 1987).

Al-Musa, Suleiman, *Ayam la Tunsa, al-Urdun fi Harab 1948* (Days That Cannot be Forgotten, Jordan in the 1948 War) (Amman: 1982).

Mustafa, Nadia Mamoud and Hiba Ra'ouf Ezzat (eds.), *Israel min eldakhil* (Israel from Within) (Cairo: Center for Political Research and Studies, 2003).

Nasr, Mohammed Abd-almu'iz, *Al-Suhyuniya fil Majal 'dawli* (Zionism in the International Arena) (Egypt: Dar al-Ma'arif, 1957).

Nye, Joseph S., *Soft Power: The Means to Success in World Politics* (New York: Public Affairs, 2004).

Podeh, Ellie, "History and Memory in the Israeli Educational System: The Portrayal of the Arab–Israeli Conflict in History Textbooks (1948–2000)", *History & Memory* 12.1 (2000).

Qahwaji, Habib, *Israel: Khanjar America* (America's Dagger) (Damascus: Mu'sast Al-'Ard, 1979).

Qashteini, Khalid, *Takween Asahyuniyah* (The Making of Zionism) (Beirut: Al-Mu'asasah Al-Arabiya Lidirasat wal Nashr, 1986).

Qutb, Sayyid, *Ma'alim fi al-Tariq* (Milestones) (Cairo: Dar al-Elshuruq, 1970).

Raswhan, Dia, "Dia, Ru'a Al-'Islam Al-Haraki" (Visions of Activist Islam), in Center for Political Research and Studies, *Egyptian Visions of Israel* (Cairo: Cairo University, 2002), pp. 57–62.

Al-Russan, Mahmud, *Ma'arik Bab al-Wad* (The Battles of Bab al-Wad) (Amman, n.d [1950?]).

Said, Abdel Monem, *al-Ahram al-Iqtisadi* (Economic Ahram), 23 January 2003.

Said, Edward W., *Orientalism: Western Conceptions of the Orient* (England: Penguin Books, 1979).

Saleem, Mohammed al-Sayid, *Al-Tahlil 'Siyasi 'Nasiri* (Nasserite Political Analysis) (Beirut: Markiz Dirasat Al-Wahda Al-'Rabyia, 1983).

Salim, Mohammed Sallah, *Al-Dimocratiya Al-Maz'umah fi Israel* (The Alleged Democracy in Israel) (Cairo: Ein for Human and Social Studies, 2002).

Sasley, Brent E., "The Role of the Arab–Israeli Conflict in Arab Domestic Policy: Using International Relations for Internal Consumption", a paper prepared for the 43rd Annual Convention of the International Studies Association, New Orleans, Louisiana, 24–27 March 2002.

Sela, Avraham, *The Decline of the Arab–Israeli Conflict: Middle East Politics and the Quest for Regional Order* (New York: State University of New York Press, 1998).

Sela, Avraham, "Arab Historiography of the 1948 War: The Quest for Legitimacy", in Laurence J. Silberstein (ed.), *New Perspectives on Israeli History: The Early Years of the State* (New York and London: New York University Press, 1991), pp. 124–54.

Shamali Nasr and Hisham Al-Dajani, *Al-Ahzab wal Kutal Asiyasyyah fi Israel* (Political Parties and Blocs in Israel) (Beirut: Maktab El-Khadamat Atiba'yah, 1986).

Shapira, Anita, *Land and Power: The Zionist Resort to Force, 1881–1948* (New York: Oxford University Press, 1992).

Sharabi, Hisham (ed.), *Theory, Politics and the Arab World: Critical Responses* (New York and London: Routledge, 1990).

Sharaf, Taha Ahmed, *Israel min Sun' 'il'sti'mar* (Israel is a Product of Colonization) (Cairo: Dar 'Ima'arif).

Shavit, Ari, "Survival of the Fittest", *Haaretz*, 8 January 2004.

Shikaki, Khalil, *Maseerah Mutaradidah Nahw 'l'tidal: Mawaqif 'Ira'I 'l'am 'lyahudi fi Israel Min 'maliyat 'salam al-Falastinia al-Israelilyah, 1980–2001* (A Hesitant Process toward Moderation: The Positions of Jewish Public Opinion in Israel Toward the Israeli–Palestinian Peace Process, 1980–2001) (Cairo: Center for Political and Strategic Studies, 2002).

Shlaim, Avi and Eugene Rogan, *The War for Palestine: Rewriting the History of 1948* (Cambridge: Cambridge University Press, 2001).

Shlaim, Avi, *War and Peace in the Middle East*, revised and updated edition (London and New York: Penguin, 1995).

Shufani, Elias, *Israel fi Khamseen 'Aman: Al-Mashru' Al-Suhyuni min Al-Mujarad Lilmalmos* (Israel in Fifty Years: the Zionist Project from the Abstract to the Concrete) (Damascus and Homs: Dar Jafra Lidrasat wal Nashr, 2002).

Singer, David, "The Level of Analysis Problem in International Relations", in Knorr Klaus and Verba Sidney (eds.), *The International System: Theoretical Essays* (Princeton, NJ: Princeton University Press, 1961), pp. 77–92.

Susser, Asher, *On Both Banks of the Jordan: A Political Biography of Wasfi Al-Tall* (London: Frank Cass, 1994)

Tawalbeh, Hassan Mohammed, *Ma'zaq Israel fi Al-Harb Wa Silim* (Israel's Predicament in War and Peace) (Beirut: Al-Mu'asasa Al-Arabiya Lidirasat Wal Nashr, 1979).

Al-Tell Abdullah, *Karitht Filastine, Mudhakarat Abdullah al-Tell, Qa'id Ma'rakat al-Quds* (The Catastrophe of Palestine, Memoirs of Abdullah al-Tell, the Leader of Jerusalem Battle) (Cairo: Dar Al-Huda, 1959).

Tessler, Mark (ed.), *Area Studies and Social Science: Strategies for Understanding Middle East Politics* (Bloomington & Indianapolis: Indiana University Press, 1999).

The Arab Human Development Report (New York: United Nations Development Programme, Regional Bureau for Arab States, 2002).

The Cultural Committee of the Editing Commission, *Hazihi 'Suhyunyiah* (This is Zionism) (Cairo: Dar al-Ma'arif, 1954).

Turner, Bryan S., *Marx and the End of Orientalism* (London: George Allen & Unwin, 1978).

Waters, Anita M., "Conspiracy Theories as Ethno-sociologies: Explanation and Intention in African American Political Culture", *Journal of Black Studies*, vol. 28, no. 1 (September 1997), pp. 112–25.

Index

— —